BOSS
OF
BUSY

BE YOUR
BEST

BOSS OF BUSY

**Combat Burn Out and
Get Clear on What Matters**

ALISON HILL

WILEY

First published as *Stand Out* in 2016 by John Wiley & Sons Australia, Ltd
42 McDougall St, Milton Qld 4064
Office also in Melbourne
This edition first published in 2019 by John Wiley & Sons Australia, Ltd

Typeset in 12.5/14.5pt Arno Pro

NATIONAL
LIBRARY
OF AUSTRALIA

A catalogue record for this
book is available from the
National Library of Australia

Internal figure designs by Kym Davis

Printed in USA by Quad/Graphics.

V224501_022619

Disclaimer
The material in this publication is of the nature of general comment only, and does not represent professional advice. It is not intended to provide specific guidance for particular circumstances and it should not be relied on as the basis for any decision to take action or not take action on any matter which it covers. Readers should obtain professional advice where appropriate, before making any such decision. To the maximum extent permitted by law, the author and publisher disclaim all responsibility and liability to any person, arising directly or indirectly from any person taking or not taking action based on the information in this publication.

For all the Catherine's, Cath's and Kate's in my world.

Contents

About the author   ix
Preface   xi
Introduction   xxi

Part I: So, who is the boss?   1
  1 Get clear on what matters   3
  2 Know your state   17

Part II: Step out of check out   29
  3 Hit the reset button   31
  4 Re-establish boundaries   45
  5 Reconnect with what matters   61

Part III: Combat burn out   79
  6 Define what's important   81
  7 Design a values-aligned life   95
  8 Defend the sacred   107

Part IV: Tackle freak out   123
  9 Map it   125
  10 Chunk it   139
  11 See it   155

Part V: Embrace stand out   171
  12 Be present   175
  13 Do it your way   187
  14 Gather your tribe   201

Conclusion   219
Boss of busy planner   225
Acknowledgements   237

About the author

Ali Hill* is Australia's coolest Psychologist. A regular in mainstream TV and print media, she is the co-founder of Pragmatic Thinking, a behaviour and motivation strategy company that carries a client list such as Pepsico, Suncorp, McDonalds, Bond University and Siemens to name a few.

Ali is the co-author of best-selling business book *Dealing with the Tough Stuff: How to achieve results from key conversations,* which has been translated into 3 languages and is in its 2nd edition. An international and in-demand keynote speaker and even more in-demand mum.

Ali is highly sought after to assist individuals, teams and organisations transition through change. She presents her unique and authentic message through engaging humour, practicality and real-world thinking,

In her spare time she turns her hand to cooking and knitting, neither of these very successfully. So Ali has decided to keep focusing on what she does best — starting a global conversation about what it takes to live a Stand Out life. It does mean there will be no home-baked goods or a knitting corner in any work she delivers ... sorry if this is a deal-breaker.

---

*   yep, here I am talking about myself in the third person. Indulge me for a second.

Preface

I was drowning. Yet the only water to be found was in the tears welling in my eyes.

The pressure I felt — in my marrow — 'twas one busy folks often feel. It was the pressure of relentless, unwavering busyness. I was drowning in an ocean of expectations, gasping for breath facing what seemed like an endless to-do list, quickly losing sight of myself and what really mattered. I could see no sign of a horizon, much less a safe harbour.

This was a feeling of slowly increasing pressure — not unusual (I mean who hasn't felt this, right?), although this time it all came to a head on one particular afternoon.

Friday, 11 April, at 3.30 in the afternoon. To. Be. Exact.

Darren, my husband, had just returned from picking up the kids from school. Pat and Kate, twin-powered tornados of seven- and five-year-old energy had whooshed through our office on their way into the house. Maybe they said 'hi', maybe they didn't — I was so consumed in my own battle for air that I didn't notice.

The shortness of breath and tightness in my chest — both physical and metaphorical — weren't eased by the infectious joy my children typically bestow on me. So often, they provide the antidote for my grown-up world, with their laughter and 'pull-my-finger' jokes; yet this time, not even them getting home could shift my thinking.

I felt antsy and anxious, positively desperate to do something, anything ... but I couldn't think of anything that could fix how I was feeling and give me what I needed — whatever it was I needed. It was Friday afternoon, after all — when others had their eyes set on the weekend, I was feeling frantic. So I defaulted; I just got busy. *I've gotta do something. What could I be doing?* I thought. *The mail! I haven't checked the mail.* Yep, the checking the mail was yet another thing I hadn't gotten round to doing yet, and was exactly what needed to happen right away.

As I stepped outside with a thundercloud, monsoon and even a bloody La Niña all hovering above my head, I rounded the corner directly into Darren, who was coming in from the car now parked in the driveway. Darren took one look at me and asked me a very simple question.

'What's wrong?'

Seriously! What is it with guys and that question? If I knew what was wrong, I'd have it fixed by now! Wouldn't I?

I stood there speechless, but in just that split-second the start of a whole discourse was taking place in my head. But rather than give voice to this internal narrative, I just stood there and glowered.

I was so disconnected from my needs and emotions that when someone I love with my whole heart asked me what was wrong, the deepest truth (which is tightly connected to our deepest fears) was that I didn't even know where to start.

No idea.

What's wrong? Darren might as well have just asked me the molecular structure of plutonium, how many litres of petrol our car takes, or to name all of the Kardashians (I can't keep up with them ...). So, of course, I went with the standard response. Through gritted teeth I said, 'I'm fine' ... and then proceeded to burst into tears (the international sign that all is not, in fact, fine). These weren't pretty-girl tears either. These were ugly tears. Reals ugly. Well, hellooo monsoon! La Niña, take a back seat for a bit, you may be needed soon ...

After I calmed a little, and through the waterfall of snot, I eventually disclosed to Daz that I wasn't coping with life. I felt like I'd lost the joy in pretty much everything I did. I distinctly remember a specific phrase I said that summed up my feelings and shocked me a little at the same time:

'I just feel like I need to opt out of life for a while.'

Now, I should be clear this wasn't a self-harm intention or statement. It was what I now refer to as a 'self-calm statement'. It was a verbal acknowledgement that things weren't right. Actually, they were very far from being right. I was drowning in the monotony of school lunches, breakfast dishes, and my personal favourite, 'What are we having for dinner?' — all while juggling a million other balls. I was losing that part of me that makes me tick, and I just didn't know how to get it back. But instead of tackling this, I just wanted to not think about any of that for a while.

Even as this declaration was spilling from my mouth, however, the diatribe in my head was also continuing: *'What have you got to whinge about?' 'You've got healthy kids' 'Your professional career is on the up' 'You're happily married to this bloke — even if he does ask infuriating questions!'*

Darren looked me square in the eye and then said something I was not expecting at all. I was expecting him to take me in his arms. Give me a hug. Tell me everything was going to be okay.

You know, do the 'man thing'. While that would have been great, today was different. He said something I couldn't have predicted, and it completely floored me.

'Babe, just have a day or two off. Do what you need to do.'

Of course, after shock, my next reaction was *Why?? Why does he want to get rid of me?*

Mentally I started checking through the likely reasons:

Did he have a speeding fine he didn't want me to know about?

Was there a boys' trip coming up he wanted brownie points for?

What time were the Eels (his favourite footy team) playing this weekend? Did he want me out of the house when they were on??

I didn't ask but looked at him quizzically and, perhaps sensing what he'd said just wasn't registering in my head, Darren repeated his sentiment. 'Do whatever you need to do. Just get away for a bit. Why don't you have the day to yourself tomorrow to do whatever you want? We'll be okay.'

Then, God love him, he did give me a hug and a kiss, and walked into the house where the kids were no doubt already causing untold carnage. (They had to be — we hadn't heard a peep from them, which any parent knows is a sure-fire sign of impending disaster.)

For what seemed like an eternity, I stood rooted to the same place in the driveway, Daz's words echoing in my head.

Just get away. Have a day to yourself. Do whatever you want.

I knew there was only one place I wanted to go: Byron Bay. Byron is a stunning coastal town in north-east New South Wales, about 40 minutes' drive from where we lived. For as long as I can remember, it has always held a strong place in my heart. It was where we used to go as kids and, as I grew older, my mum and I used to go for walks along the beach there — long walks; even longer talks. Using Mum's favourite word, those beaches, that place; it's ... special.

For me, the calming presence that was Byron had been a part of my upbringing. Only in later years would I come to realise the area carries a deeper mystery — and not just the hippie/boho business it is often associated with these days, but also something more ancient and spiritual. The traditional custodians of the Byron area, the Indigenous Arakwal people, have known for thousands of years that Byron was a place of healing. At that moment on my driveway, I needed healing, and not just for a cut or scratch, but for something deeper and more visceral than that.

While the decision about where to go was easy, however, the decision to actually go was harder.

When Darren said, 'Why don't you have the day to yourself?' half of me was going, 'Yeah, baby! See ... you ... later!' and the other half was screaming, 'Are you serious? I can't just up and go, that kinda thing's gotta be planned, I've got things to do, I don't deserve it, just suck it up princess!'

It's safe to say my pillow endured a lot of tossing and turning that night as I wrest the decision from one point to the next. Despite all my angst about going, I got up early the following morning (before I could talk myself out of it), packed my bag and drove down the Pacific Highway from our home on the Gold Coast to the golden beaches of Australia's eastern-most point.

About fifteen minutes into the drive, along a stretch of the Pacific Highway that cuts through the sugar cane fields with the majestic Mount Warning on the horizon, a tunnel comes up just after the small township of Chinderah. Now you might be thinking, *How does she recall a goddamn tunnel? Who is this chick, a female version of 'Rain Man'?* Trust me, when you have two little kids, and there are very few tunnels around, you know exactly where they are.

As I was driving through that tunnel, I paid attention to just how noisy my head had been for the entire trip. Here's just a taste of what was running through my head:

Who do you think you are?!

You don't have enough money for this.

You still have to lose that last 5 kilograms before you go.

Why did you leave the house in a mess like that?

The kids need a haircut. You can't even sort out your family when you're home, what use are you being away?

Who do you think you are??!!

It was horrible. Not the house or the family — they were fine — but, rather, the way I was treating myself. That was the only awful thing going on. Here I was, beating myself up for even going. I was experiencing every flavour of guilt, including the worst flavour — parental guilt. I mean, seriously — who just gets up one morning and leaves their young kids to go off and do their own thing? This was the kind of self-deprecating angst I was putting myself through.

Thankfully, as I drove out of that tunnel I thought, *This is ridiculous* and I gave myself a pep talk that even Tony Robbins would have been proud of. And yep, I did it out loud, in the car, on my own:

Alison, you're doing it. There's no point debating whether it's a good idea. You're in the car driving ... just be okay with that.

Then I did what all good-intended, guilt-ridden, busy people do. I started negotiating with myself:

Right, well; it's 8 am now. I'll be in Byron by 8.30 am. I'll do a perfect parallel park outside the local bookstore before I grab an insightful book, a journal and the perfect pen. Then I'll stroll past the shops down to the beach where I'll sit reflectively in lotus pose and contemplate. My big epiphany and 'A-ha!' moment will happen precisely at 11.15 am and what I need to do to get sorted will be clear. Then I'll drive home to tell Darren how successful I've been in pulling myself together, getting back in time to bring in the washing and make the kids dinner.

Seriously!! I couldn't even have a day off to relax without planning it with military precision! Arrggghhh. Enough.

Walking out the door of my house wasn't easy, but what faced me right then was something monumentally harder. On that drive to Byron Bay — in that moment — I hadn't realised that I was going to discover the true reason for my dispirited, downtrodden soul. It wasn't my life. It wasn't the kids, work or even the friggin Kardashians.

It was me.

Bam. Ouch.

I was my biggest barrier. I'd been worried about the kids, the house, the business, if my cycle was aligned with the moon's ... but I'd never thought about whether I could be the problem. So I made a decision right there. No more blame placed on everything else. This was just me here. The kids were okay and Darren was okay; it was just me. And if I wanted better, it started with treating myself better.

I made a pact with myself. I would do whatever I wanted when I got to Byron. No plans, no lists, no mental progress chart. I'd lie on the beach if I wanted to. I'd get a massage if I wanted to. Hell, I'd eat as much over-priced organic food as I wanted to.

And that's what I did. I walked on the beach. I swam. I listened to music but, mostly, I just listened to me. While the letting go was hard, the recuperation was bliss. And you know what else I did? I rang Darren in the afternoon and told him I wanted to stay and that I'd booked a motel for the night.

His reply? 'No worries.'

For a split-second I got anxious again. His response was far too nonchalant for my liking. But I realised that was just the fear part of my brain. Of course, it'd be okay. And so I stayed the night. Slept. Ate. Walked. Swam. Repeat.

And this food for my soul was divine — and it was over in a blink.

Truthfully, when I arrived home after this time away — this brief opt-out — I was wondering what I'd be walking back into. Will I see my kids drowning in piles of washing similar to when they are in the ball pit at Ikea? Will every single dish we own be piled dangerously high in the sink? Will my husband be curled up in a corner gently sobbing??

I pulled up in the driveway (the scene of my meltdown only 48 hours earlier), opened the door to the house, and ... Nothing. Everything was completely fine! And not 'fine' like 'woman fine', like actually fine. The kids were happy, hubby gave me a kiss, and I even found a clean cup for an organic sleepy-time tea (which a sleepy looking hippy in Byron talked me into buying). Everything was — well, like, totally fine.

And there lay more clarity for me. The world genuinely didn't care what I thought, said or did. It just kept on keeping on. It never asked for permission. My choice on how I interacted with my world is my choice.

So there it was. I'd had to confront two blinding realities in the space of two days. First, I was my own biggest hurdle to happiness (ouch) and, second, I — and no-one else — held the keys to finding my own health, calm and love. This second reality was tremendously empowering. And downright farrrking scary.

You see, what I'd had a reminder of is that when we fully own ourselves — and every last bit of ourselves, not just the good bits but also the messy bits — we have the foundation to live a Stand Out life.

To be honest, I already knew this stuff. After working as a counsellor and psychologist for more than fifteen years, I knew rationally how this stuff worked. I'm a professional head-mechanic and I'm good at what I do — I'd given some damn good advice over the years. But we all know that theory and practice can be separate entities, and here presented the most difficult client I'd faced: me.

So I became my own patient, and I worked on me. I journalled, did yoga, had acupuncture, saw a therapist, got angry, cried, shouted and went quiet. But above all, I stayed patient and compassionate. Along the way, I noticed more and more people feeling how I had felt on that Friday afternoon. I became obsessed with how we can live extraordinary and outrageously fulfilled lives, even among the busyness of our world.

Among the quagmire of emotions, inner monologues, trials and tribulations, I was able to identify — based on a platform of science — the patterns that derail our success, and the twin pathways that can supercharge your magnificence. As I examined my own experiences against a mountain of books, journals and research papers, a foundation started to emerge; and as I correlated the commonalities faced by my clients, further patterns emerged and announced themselves. And these patterns made perfect sense in a sometimes senseless world.

Our pursuit together, as you read this book, is to find a different way. You'll find a space where you can get clear on what matters. And, yep, I'm quite aware how intoxicating that sounds — and how terrifying it can make you feel at the same time.

This is a call to arms to fight for something better.

To play big instead of playing small.

To love harder — so damn hard it scares you.

To become the boss of busy, embrace self-expression and stop bowing to the pressure of urgency.

And we'll do it by combining both purpose and progress in the mundane as well as the big things in life.

This is your time, so let's get cracking, eh?

Love

Ali x

Introduction

Life sure is messy. And, honourably, the messier it gets, the more we try to organise it, control it and make it manageable — which itself is busy work. When we're in this frame of mind, we wake up in the morning, world rushing at us, throw a coffee over our worries and rip in — continually driven by a belief that life wouldn't be this messy if we were more organised, fitter, smarter; if we just had it all together.

So we pile up our to-do list higher than a teenage boy's dinner plate at an all-you-can-eat buffet. Paradoxically, this puts us under even more pressure, and feeling more overwhelmed with all the things we have to do. The pressure of trying to keep it together while we stem the tide of messy becomes too much. But don't you dare drop any of those balls you're juggling!

Get busier. Try harder. That's the answer. Or is it?

Let's take a little sneaky peek at the results: we're overloaded, tired, stressed, tired, busy, tired, exhausted ... did I say tired? And the impact of this is being felt across the board. In her book *The Sleep Revolution*, Arianna Huffington (co-founder and editor-in-chief of *The Huffington Post*) highlights that *#tired* has been used over 27 million times on Instagram, and if you type 'why am I so ...' into a Google search, the most common end to this sentence is 'tired'. Globally, we're all desperate to find a way out of weary.

We need to face facts: we are stuffing up our lives by trying to work harder at working hard. This intent, seemingly noble on the surface, is a sure-fire way of losing your health, happiness and sanity. We need a different approach — one that doesn't cost us these essential components of our lives, and something that's more than just working harder.

Open 24/7

We live in a time where 'open 24/7' has been sold to us as a convenience. And in a lot of ways it is. We now are able to go to the gym and pump weights at 2 am if we want to, bop down the aisles of the local supermarket to Richard Marx's greatest hits long after the rush hour has kicked in, and scream into the pharmacy for an urgent order of fungal cream whenever we want (okay that last one is actually quite convenient). When we find ourselves on the couch, we can watch whatever we want, whenever we want, rather than viewing times being dictated to us by the networks. And who doesn't love a good Netflix binge-watch? Our world is like a giant remote control.

Play. Rewind. Fast forward. Play again. But the pause button? She's-a-broken.

This ease of convenience has crossed over into our connectivity and communications. The flexibility in how we interact, when we interact and who we interact with around the globe has fundamentally changed the way that we connect with each other, including random strangers who can be granted our time and attention at the expense of those in front of us. (C'mon, you've surely whiled away a couple of hours of your precious time in some sort of Facey-post 'serve-volley-return', haven't you?)

So while this connectivity has brought us many bonuses, it has also come with a few downsides, and perhaps the most obvious downside is the intrusion on our time. While we have more demands within our day, the parameters haven't changed. We still have only 24 hours in a day, and 7 days in a week. You can't do anything that will give you bonus hours. If you waste a day, you don't have hours striped from you. You've got 24 hours, in 60-minute lots. That's your quota. Something has to take a hit and wear the cost of stretching this time too far. The collateral damage is a collective feeling of overwhelm in our society that means we are constantly running in a million different directions. The fight for your attention is real: the project, the mother-in-law, the chocolate cake sitting in the communal fridge at work. Couple this feeling with the relentless change environment that we are now facing, particularly in our places of work, and the result is higher exhaustion levels and shorter fuses. Within the corporate world, organisations no longer speak about five year plans — because they don't know what the lay of the land is going to be in five months' time, let alone five years. Change is absolutely relentless and individuals are merely holding on.

Phew! Have I cheered you up? *#sorrynotsorry*

Among this busyness we find that we snap quicker than we should, we disconnect from the people we love the most, and we get caught up doing what we think we should be doing, leaving what we want to be doing at the bottom of the pile — gathering dust because we keep adding to the pile. As a result, we end up consumed by fear, worry and guilt about postponing the things that really matter to us — and then trying to numb the despair we feel. Busy is the boss and we're its faithful servants, turning up full pelt whenever it snaps its fingers. Losing sleep, losing our mind, and losing connection to what we truly love. This, ultimately, has an impact on our health, our happiness and our sanity.

Is any of this resonating with you? If you're nodding your head like one of those dashboard bobble-head thingos, it's okay. You're not alone — and it doesn't have to always be like this.

Becoming the boss of busy

As a psychologist I connect with people every day who are drowning in expectations. Before going into this any further, though, I first want you to check the mental picture you have going on in your head of a psych with a client. You might be thinking leather couches, inkblot butterflies or people incoherently babbling while being surrounded by empty Doritos packets. Well, nope. The people I work with are achieving amazing things. They're nailing projects, leading teams and workplaces into the future, and running families like ninja warriors — from the outside, there's not a straightjacket in sight. Their lives look normal; successful, complete, even. But inside it looks decidedly different — because on the inside, they're screaming for it all to stop. For someone to notice their desperation.

They are hoping that their time to jump off the treadmill, even for a moment, comes soon. These are the people sitting next to you on the train; one could be the person in the cubicle next to yours or the neighbour you pass as you put out the bins. This is me, you, him and her. We recognise the screams and cries for help because we've added to the choir. We've drunk (gorged ourselves, actually) at the fountain of too much, and then felt the ache for relief. But it hasn't arrived and what's left ain't pretty.

**EVEN WHEN WE ARE BEING PULLED
IN A MILLION DIFFERENT DIRECTIONS,
WE CAN FEEL CALM IN THE CHAOS.
WE CAN MOVE FROM MARTYR TO CENTRED,
AND FROM BEING 'OVER IT' TO 'I'M ALL OVER IT'.**

Rather than continue the horror story that plays out in your mirror, I can assure you this: through science-based research I've identified a different path towards a fulfilled life we can walk on; actually, we can bloody well stride on it with the stride of a warrior — confident and purposeful with power. We can take big leaping bounds, not driven through fear, pressure or haste. Even when we are being pulled in a million different directions, we can feel calm in the chaos. We can move from martyr to centred, and go from being 'over it' to 'I'm all over it'. We can put busy in its place, telling it to take a back seat for a while.

Yep, that's right — we can become the boss of busy rather than the other way round. Truth.

What would it be like for you if you had these moments of clarity even among the busyness? What if, even when life was rushing at you (sometimes in the form of a toddler with a spoonful of porridge aimed directly at your freshly ironed work shirt moments before you step out the door on your way to a major presentation), you could re-centre, reconnect and come back to what's really important? What would it feel like to rise above the noise and turn up feeling calm, focused and clear on what's important to your day? Huh?

Imagine having clarity about what really mattered to you at any given moment, and being able to make decisions based on that, rather than what's urgent (or at least someone else's urgent).

Imagine being excited about the progress you were making towards those things that truly matter. Even in the moments when it feels like the goal-posts have shifted, significantly — not just to another postcode but to another country — imagine being able to straighten up, grit your teeth and summon another effort. Like a boss. It'd be rad, don't you think?

And, let's face it: the alternative sucks balls. Being in a rut. Ergh.

What the research shows is that one of the unhealthiest places human beings can find themselves is feeling stuck.

Despair shows up when we fundamentally believe that nothing will change, and that tomorrow is going to be exactly like today.

So let's make a deal. Let's tell that rut you've found yourself in that you're moving out. The lease is up and it can find itself a new tenant. Because when you truly break free of that feeling of being stuck, it's, well ... beautiful. The grass is greener and the sky is bluer. Having belief and evidence that tomorrow is going to be different is such a powerful force it's a life-changer. But let's not get ahead of ourselves thinking about double rainbows and frolicking in pastures watered by unicorn tears. Let's stay grounded because we have much work to do.

What if nothing changed?

Take a moment to take stock of your life right here and now. You've picked up this book for a reason. Something tweaked your interest — even if it was just, 'What's this crazy psychologist got to say that I haven't already heard before?'

Well, I have a starting question for you, and it's a biggie.

As you consider your life and the stressors you feel on a daily basis, consider the relationships you have, and consider that growing to-do list that consumes and eclipses the pile of 'damn-I-wish-I-could' items. After considering all this, now think about this:

If nothing were to change for you, what would that mean?

Sure, it sounds a little crazy, but really taking some time to pick at the seams of this question is worthwhile. What would it mean if things kept going as they are? What would it mean in five months' time? What would it mean in five years' time? Take a few minutes, grab a pen and piece of paper, and jot down a couple of words that come to mind for you.

Perhaps you're thinking, *You know what, Ali? Life's pretty good and I'm really happy with it.* Awesome. Skim-read this book and pat yourself on the back when you read something that makes you think, *Yep, got that covered!* Keep moving forward, keep making progress and connect it to what matters. You can look for the occasional titbit to help you even more with the stuff you love doing. You're on fire. Keep at it.

On the other hand, if your response is more like a soul-sinking *Oh-hell-no/I don't want to sit in this fear, mess and despair anymore/This is not good enough, not yet,* now's the time for a reframe. Remember: self-calm, not self-harm.

This soul-sinking feeling now becomes your drive, your reason to do the required work. This is the motivation to ask yourself, 'Where am I going to make changes?' and 'How am I going to turn up even when it's really difficult?'

If this sounds like you, we have work to do. It's not easy work and I can't give you a silver bullet that will cure it all overnight, but if you're ready to go through the hard stuff, I can tell you it will reward you. Therefore, read on, you adventurer of spirit. Let's step through this together.

What state are you in?

When a house is on fire, those professional firefighters get to work on putting out the fire. They don't stand there pontificating about the likely causes of the fire or who is at fault. Their task is urgent. They back the truck up, flex their muscles, grab their hoses and get to work.

But once the fire is out, the other work still needs to happen. Once the urgency has passed, the fire investigators need to come in and determine the reasons for the fire. And while their insights can't magically reverse the tragic event of a house burning down, if the investigators didn't come in after the fire was out, we'd never see changes to aspects such as building standards or efforts put into building evacuations. The truth is the high-pressure, rapid work of fire-fighting has saved countless lives, but the number of lives saved through carefully considered investigative methods and reporting is unimaginably more.

Sure, for some elements in your life you won't have the time to ask the real question about how you can work better, lead better, handle this situation differently. You'll just need to put the fire out. Now. Toddler running towards a busy road? No time to review your parenting skills, just grab that anklebiter! Work project due in six hours and your computer crashes? No time to research the latest laptop options and customer reviews, just get the damn thing in!

But (and this is a super-big but) you can't let everything become urgent. A part of you is yearning for the time and space to deal with the big, important issues. So let's not have that swamped. The onus is on you to make this space. My intent is that this book provides you with the permission to do that.

We're going to explore a new possibility, from new ways of facing your day, managing your tasks, and taming your voice.

This book is broken into five parts. The first part addresses that whisper that occasionally builds into a roar, that question that rears its ugly head when it seems the whole world is going batshit-crazy (or when we can't see what to do next) — how do I get my shit together?

Once we've covered getting your shit together (GYST) in part I, we'll go through a simple self-diagnostic to help you identify what to focus on now to move away from three oft-felt cognitive states:

> » *Check Out:* the sense that you don't actually belong in your world, along with the feeling that your contribution is without worth, and the simplest way to stop the pain is to turn up physically but not invest too much mentally or emotionally.

» *Burn Out:* the feeling you are on a treadmill that is dialled too fast for your legs, your brain and your talents to keep pace with, and that you'll fall down at any given moment. You dare not stop, though, if one ball drops then all might come crashing down; so you just hold on tight.

» *Freak Out:* that overriding anxiety generated by having found a sense of direction, but feeling like you're struggling to take meaningful steps forward.

And you know what? If you read those three states and thought *Omergawd. I'm in all three!*, that's perfectly fine. Because I'm going to show you how to move from Check Out, Burn Out or Freak Out to a state that's much, much better: Stand Out.

So the remaining four parts of this book (parts II to V) will focus on key actions when we're in these four states. And the three chapters within each of these parts highlight the three key actions for each of the states. This book is your guide to these four states, but the reality is all of us spend time in all of the states. So when you find yourself in any of these states, use this book to work your way through them. This is your compass when you're in the rough seas.

In many chapters you'll also come across a 'life hack'. These life hacks are practical challenges based on psychological research and are opportunities to jolt the broken record of your current behaviours and step into new behaviours. These life hacks may stretch you, and in some cases you may even want to dismiss them, saying something like, 'That'll never work for me'. But let's cut a deal. If you give them a go, I'll promise not to say 'I told yer so!' when they do work. You see, the actions and suggestions within this book aren't plucked from the sky; they're born of science. They work. And if you're ever in doubt, dial up your curiosity for something different. Maybe, just maybe, another approach would be interesting to explore. There is great truth in the old adage, 'If you do what you've always done, you'll get what you've always got'. Lean into these challenges and consider the learnings that arise for you — something just might shift as you do.

It's your time to Stand Out

So, I have a confession to make. I listen to Keith Urban (by choice), and sometimes I fart while doing yoga. Okay, that was two confessions but, hey, I figured we've gotten to know each other by now. *#BFFs #deepandmeaningful*

I'm a really long way from living the perfect life. But I wouldn't swap it for all the shoes in Carrie Bradshaw's walk-in wardrobe. Seriously, how did we get to this point where we need everything to be perfect before we can start? The house, the clothes, the car, the waistline, the white teeth; if we just wait till they're all perfect, then I can get about the task of being awesome. But it's a furphy, fool's gold and a mirage all wrapped up in one. *Now* is the time to stand out — like, this very second.

Typically, I come across amazing men and women who hold themselves back because they're not sure if it's their time. They're afraid of push back, of being judged, of being isolated from their peers and loved ones. Of course, to change oneself is to be different from the norm, so we fit in. Stay the same. Join the herd.

Being invited to stand out is scary, and it's easier to not do it; to let others have the limelight and shelve our own plans for awesomeness until we're really ready. In some ways, it is easy to see why we default to helping others in front of ourselves. We get so much by giving to others, and by lifting them up.

Here's the thing, though: it's not mutually exclusive. Scarcity thinking makes us believe it is, but we live in abundance. We can do both things. We can stand out in our life *and* lift others up. In fact, we owe it to the men and women who come after us to stand out. Wouldn't you want your daughter to know that it's possible to feel comfortable in a space that has previously been held only for the 'boys' clubs', for example, and to stand on her own two feet, comfortable in her own skin? Wouldn't you want your son to have the confidence to say when it's all too much and find his way back healthily from the brink of pressure?

I wrote this book for my daughter, who is strong-willed, spirited, adventure-loving and curious, and whose gifts to the world need to be shared. I wrote this book for my mum, who set the example of how showing vulnerability is one of the hardest endeavours, and the only thing that truly ties us together (even when it's tough and others don't like what they see in the mirror). I wrote this book for my son, whose kind heart will be threatened by an archaic macho male culture's attempts to harden it, yet who will be capable of flipping the tables and becoming a leader of men through love, not force, if he chooses.

And, ultimately, I wrote this book for you. It's your turn to stand out, to be the boss, but you won't be alone. A tsunami of people is in your corner cheering you on, ready for you to step out of the shadows.

This work is not easy. You can't just do it once and then sit back and admire your creation. You need to sign up for the long haul. If that's not you right now, if this change is not important enough to you yet, shut this book, hand it to a friend or let it gather dust till you're ready. But if you're prepared to do hard things (which you are infinitely capable of doing, by the way), let's roll up our sleeves and get to it. The rewards at the other end may just blow your mind.

Part I
So, who is the boss?

Overwhelm hits us, and it hits hard. Sometimes it's the slow pressure cooker, building up over time before bursting from our mouths in a tirade just because the little red man at the crossing light seems to be taking forever to give us a turn (seriously, some days he just seems to be messing with us for sport). Other times, overwhelm happens in a defined, specific moment. The flood comes all at once and knocks the wind out of us in an instant.

In these moments of overwhelm you might find yourself whispering, 'Oooohhh, I've just gotta get my shit together'. Occasionally that whisper comes out as a scream, with a few superlatives attached to it for greater effect.

While productivity sounds like what we've got to dial up, often the reality is that focusing purely on being more productive adds fuel to the fire of overwhelm — with a side order of guilt. The pathway out of feeling overloaded is to come back to the why and the what. Why this and what's next? This then leads into an understanding of the four states, and which one (or ones) you might be in.

CHAPTER 1
Get clear on what matters

Wouldn't it be lovely to say goodbye to the weight of overwhelm, the pressure of expectations and the barrage of busyness that wears you down? How good would it be to jump off the conveyor belt of chaos? But when? Seriously, who's got time for that? Do you got that nagging feeling that if you stop running — even for a second — life will swamp you in a deluge?

This sense of overwhelm comes from two places. First, we're overwhelmed because of our uncertainty about what to do next. Which decision should I make that will be 'right', how do I find balance, should I have red quinoa or white quinoa? (Seriously, even a quick trip to the supermarket results in many mini-meltdown moments!) Second, overwhelm comes from wanting to do it all. With so many options and so many ideas that we want to dive into feet first, we're burning the midnight oil and getting swamped in our own busyness.

Consumed by the sheer amount of what needs to be done, and underneath not really sure where we sit in it all, we can feel like we're doing it all on our own. For me, this is where my inner martyr turns up, stepping in to insist, 'I've got this', 'No, let me', 'I'll take it *all* on and just suck it up'. My inner martyr definitely works solo — if you offer her help, she'll flatly refuse; get offended even. Then she'll storm off in a huff just to prove to you that she's got this. The louder and more frequent the huffs, the more she's telling you to back away (while actually silently screaming for help).

In the moments of feeling over it and stuck in a deep rut without a single off-ramp in sight, we cling to anything that will make us feel better. Busyness leads to bargaining, self-sacrifice and hours of researching how you can have a coffee-machine intravenously attached to you just to get through the day (or maybe that's just me). This is why we whisper to ourselves, under our breath, 'I've gotta get my shit together'. Maybe you shout it out loud. Regularly. Like hourly. Every. Day.

If you're nodding agreement, you're in the right place.

These whispers are your impetus for change. Change only occurs, though, when you are clear about what needs to change.

Let's check the pulse

Things can be different — and making changes doesn't have to be all about giving things up, regrets and caffeine by the bucketload. But the only way things will be different is if you first recognise where you're at, right here and now. It's time to look at what's really going on.

So, let's take some time to check our 'pulse'. Not your actual pulse; I'm sure yours is fine (a little hurried maybe, but still operating). Besides, the whole this-is-a-book-and-I-can't-actually-check-your-real-pulse thing kinda gets in the way. No, let's check the pulse of busyness in your world and its impact.

Take some time with a pen and paper and go through the following questions, rating yourself on where you currently sit on the described continuums.

The Boss of Busy scale

Where are you at? (Rate yourself from 1 to 10.)

1. How often do you take time out to hit the reset button for yourself?

1
'Time out? That'll happen when I'm dead.'

10
'Every day is "me" day.'

2. Do the people closest to you know what your no-go zones are?

1
'I'm the master of saying yes when I don't mean it.'

10
'My boundaries are like the Great Wall of China — so clear you can see them from space.'

3. If someone asks you what your strengths are, what is your response?

1
'The only thing I'm good at is second-guessing myself ... I think? Um ... what do you think?'

10
'I can rattle off what I rock at in a heartbeat.'

4. Do you know the things that really, truly matter to you?

1
'I used to but they've become lost under the busyness.'

10
'At any given moment I know what's important.'

5. How clear are you on exactly what your values are?

1
'Family, health, happiness are my go-to boring responses.'

10
'I'm razor-sharp clear on my unique values.'

6. Do the people around you know exactly what presses your buttons?

1   10
'I'm the enigma.'   *'I'm the open book.'*

7. How mapped out are the goals you want to achieve?

1   10
'I've bought myself a planner, but   *'They're mapped out to within an*
it's gathering dust.'   *inch of their lives.'*

8. How obvious is the next step you need to take?

1   10
'All I do is react to what's right in   *'What's next is clear to me and*
front of me.'   *takes priority.'*

9. When it comes to planning your week or day, do your happiness and health make it onto the to-do list?

1   10
'They're always the bottom of the   *'These things are the first in the*
pile, last priority.'   *calendar.'*

10. How visible are your goals and values?

1   10
'They're in my head, does that   *'They smack me in the face*
count?'   *wherever I go.'*

11. How comfortable are you with failure?

1   10
'Failure is only for losers.'   *'Failure is proof I'm pushing the*
boundaries.'

12. Do you have people around you who both challenge you and back you?

1	10
'Does my goldfish count?'	*'My tribe are on speed-dial.'*

Remember as you take yourself through these questions: no-one is going to know your answers. This is one of those places where you don't have to respond based on what you think you 'should' say or what others would expect from you. Shake that off and go through the questions again with an honest lens. No bullshit; warts 'n' all truth. Focus especially on the areas that make you wince with awareness because they've touched a nerve — now is the time to stare that reality in the face. These should become your personal focus points throughout the rest of the book.

They've sold us a lemon

For a long time we've been sold the magic pill of productivity. It'll combat overwhelm quicker than a rattlesnake's strike, we're told. This 'ere elixir will cure yer arthritis, bronchitis, cellulitis and any other 'itis you may have. It's snake oil for the stressed soul.

We've been told that we just need to learn time management skills to be more efficient and be able to get more done in a shorter amount of time. But it's a hoax. A massive myth you should stop buying into. It's not that time management strategies don't work; it's that they work when you're already good at time management. The results of this three-decade-old directive are now clearly evident in how people are feeling: overwhelmed. And that's despite there being some fantastic productivity tips and tools out in the market.

Back in the 1980s we were also sold that multi-tasking was the key — that is, being able to do not just one thing but five things at once. We needed to diversify our skills. This may have been a great idea for workplaces, but it was a terrible idea for our brains. Research is now finding that our brain is incapable of multi-tasking. Instead of attending to multiple tasks, our brains have been shown on MRI scans to be rapidly switching between two tasks. In this rapid attention splitting, our brains get fatigued and we experience a lag in reorientation when we come back to a task. If you've ever been absorbed in something and then gotten distracted, you'll have experienced how tough that initial moment of getting back into the task is. When we think we're multi-tasking we're actually not really doing any of the tasks well.

Tied in with our orienting response system, this multi-tasking uses up a lot of juice — have you ever had those days when you've been juggling a million balls, yet feel like you've achieved nothing? On the other hand, how good do you feel after a day when you've had a singular focus on something important? It's energising, isn't it? With the multi-tasking myth buried, the considered approach is now all about the power of mindfully being fully present in the one thing that we're doing.

'But surely, Ali,' you may say, 'the answer to me getting on top of things is to get cracking, and be more productive?' Look, I know we've been drinking from that well for a long, long time, but perhaps I can shift your thoughts by looking forensically at the word 'productivity'. In the word's definition, we find the key to why it is not the answer to our overwhelm. Productivity is defined as a per unit measure of efficiency.

This definition makes sense back in the Industrial era where what many people did was work in factories with the goal of getting more of the exact same product out the door in the same amount of time. A productivity guru's dream. The focus was on having machines (and people) work more efficiently so there was more productivity in the same amount of time.

The truth is in this current world, however, not every email is created equal. Not every phone call that we make is the same. The goal is not to do more emails. The goal is not to spend the whole day on the phone. The goal should be about the quality of the conversations we have. It should be about connecting with the right people, at the right time, in the right way — that opens up doors for us. It's not about getting more done in a shorter amount of time because, as evidence shows, that just leaves us exhausted at the end of the day, collapsing on the couch, with the only looming possibility being that we have to get up and do the exact same thing tomorrow. The cold, hard truth is that strategy trumps productivity hands down.

Interestingly, through further exploration of the definition of productivity we can view the actual origin of the word 'produce'. And it's killer. Damn thing stopped me in my tracks, and since then, I've related this to thousands of people in presentations at various conferences.

THE COLD, HARD TRUTH IS THAT STRATEGY TRUMPS PRODUCTIVITY HANDS DOWN.

Produce comes from the Latin *prōdūcere*, which means to bring forward, bring forth or bring into existence. So 'to produce' means 'to bring into being'.

As I read those words, something shifted in me. It resonated to my core. Because 'bring into being' can relate to any work or activity you are doing. Playing with the kids isn't about being productive, but about 'bringing into being' their growth and development. Spending time on a spreadsheet for a project is about 'bringing into being' accountability and structure to get the job done. 'Bringing into being' is about creating something that wasn't there before, something that is unique because it's got your fingerprint on it. To me, this dovetails perfectly with the intent of this book: the need to gain clarity on purpose and step forward with progress.

Typically when I ask people about their goals, hopes and dreams, their response isn't about doing more — it's about doing better, leaving a legacy. And what they want to do better wholly centres on what they are trying to bring into being. The thing that wasn't there before.

My question for you is: What are you bringing into being? What are you creating that either wasn't there before, or is different because you are doing it? What has your fingerprint on it in a way that no-one else could do? What are you bringing into being that has your DNA on it? What's that thing you want to create?[1]

Your creation could be something tangible like writing a book, planting a herb garden or getting a finisher's medallion at a half-marathon. Or perhaps your creation is less tangible, but no less important. It might be a ritual to bring you closer to your children, working on your mindset to further your career or perhaps it's dreaming up a way to surprise and delight your partner. Tangible or intangible, these things are art. They fill your soul with light. They are yours to create; to bring into being. Remember: it's simply not about how we can get more done in a shorter space of time; it's about what it is that you can step into.

But we need to navigate a few roadblocks along our way to bringing our best to the world. The biggest one? Our fear that it might not work.

---

1 Okay, that was more than one question; I got on a roll.

What if I fail?

This is the point when we start searching for a guarantee. We start thinking, *If I'm going to bring into being something that is new, that hasn't been created yet, something that I'll be putting my reputation on the line for, it had better be good. No. Perfect. Otherwise, what's the point?*

This fear permeates our thinking. What sits behind the fear is the belief that if we're going to produce something and bring it into being:

» it has to be perfect

» it can't be judged, criticised or pulled down

» I have to do it all on my own or else it doesn't count.

Talk about piling on the pressure. Let's put these beliefs under the microscope.

First, when you are bringing something into being, waiting until it's perfect is a brilliant procrastination tool. Through the lens of perfectionism, we hold ourselves back, obsess about the details that often don't really matter, or sometimes not even start in the first place. The world is moving too fast for us to wait until we reach perfect. The notion of perfect is elusive anyway. Becoming okay with the discomfort of producing, and sharing what you've produced before it's perfect is key to living a Stand Out life. In fact, it's a requirement. Sometimes what you produce connects and resonates with others because of its imperfections. We bring things into being in order to serve others, and recognising this can help you overcome your fear of it not being perfect.

The second sabotaging fear is of being judged, criticised or pulled down. When we bring something into being we want to ensure that we get five-star reviews every time. Guess what? You won't. When you put yourself out there, when you rattle the cages, others will judge, maybe criticise, perhaps even pull you down. The more you stand out, and the more that you produce in life, the more you'll be in the firing line.

These words cut deeply, and they can bring forth our deepest fears. However, this critique and finger pointing often has very little to do with you, and usually says more about the other person and what they feel uncomfortable with.

Remember this: criticism is unavoidable when you produce, so stop waiting for a time when criticism will go away. People will have their opinions, and people will have their say. This doesn't make your courage any less, nor your impact any less important.

The third sabotaging belief is that to produce something, to put our name to it, we have to own all of it. It's our job to do every single part of the process — otherwise, we can't claim it. This is our internal martyr.

All the great things that have ever been achieved, and the people who we believe are successful, all have a trail of people behind them who support them. The belief that we have to do all of it is one that needs to be shed.

FAILING IS OKAY. REGRET BECAUSE YOU NEVER STARTED IS NOT.

'So what if I fail?' When that question pops up, confront the sabotaging belief and remember that in order to bring into being that thing that you need to create, nowhere is it written that it has to be perfect, it has to dodge criticism, or you have to slave it out on your own without any help.

Failing is okay. Regret because you never started is not.

Meeting the two drivers of change

Working with individuals, teams and organisations through transitions and change is the common thread that ties together the different paths of my career, and this I know: change is hard.

How we transition through periods of change can make or break us. Those who lose their way in the transition through change often are stuck and stagnated.

Losing your way through change comes about because of two main reasons:

1. You lose sight of the bigger purpose.

2. You stop making progress.

These challenges give us the clue to the two main drivers for change. Our ammunition to strike back at busy. But first, have a think about the following and the feelings they bring up:

» How do you turn up at work when you are stressed and under the pump?

» How do you respond to that team meeting that drags on longer than it should?

» How do you turn up to your family, friends or kids when you are feeling like this?

It's kinda like the next person who comes within a 5-metre radius could get their head bitten off, isn't it?! Seriously, what are they even doing??

Compare these feelings to when you are feeling calm, able to breathe and your coping cup (yes, that's a technical term) is full.

How do you turn up at your work and with family now?

While the situations are the same (you're damn busy), what you bring to the situation drastically changes not only your experience but also the impact you have on others.

Sure, we all get stressed from time to time. Busy takes over and sets up camp — ignoring our subtle hints to pack its bag and leave. Unless we've got some strategies to combat busy, the bugger keeps winning. The key to finding out what these strategies are lies in these two drivers of change.

DRIVER 1: CONNECTING TO PURPOSE

The first driver for combating busy is having a sense of purpose — that thing that lights you up, that's important to you, that you can't not do.

We do so many things in our life that are just automatic, where we're going through the motions — for example, parking in the same zone at a shopping centre every time we go there (regardless of whether the shop we want today is at completely the other end).

When we lose sight of purpose we are doing what everyone else is doing because we believe that's what needs to be done. What I hear from individuals in organisations who have disconnected from the 'why' is statements that involve, 'just because'. Why do you have a team meeting every Tuesday at 8:30 am? 'Oh, just because it's what we've always done. It's just the way things are done around here.' This important disconnect from why meetings and why this time has two causes: time fades the original intent because you haven't come back to why this is important, and there wasn't a strong enough purpose in the first place (it's just what other organisations do).

Simon Sinek is an American author and speaker whose TED Talk and subsequent bestselling book *Start with Why* skyrocketed the conversation about the power of connecting to purpose. Sinek suggested when individuals and brands focus on their why first, and share this with others, they inspire others. Connection and trust happen fast when we share our stories of 'why'.

Having a sense of purpose sits on a continuum (see figure 1.1). Up the higher end of the continuum is where we 'know why'. We have a clear reason and that reason leaves us with a certain strut and purpose in our step.

Down the lower end of the continuum is where there's 'no why'. We're going through the process because it's what we think we 'should' be doing, or it's what other people have done, so it must work.

NO WHY ——— ——— —— **KNOW WHY**

Figure 1.1: purpose continuum

We can have a clear sense of purpose in certain areas of our life but not in others. For example, you're ready to run a 10-kilometre event because that's a clear part of your fitness goals, but when it comes to financial goals you're just paying off the house because that's what needs to be done.

While purpose is important, purpose alone doesn't get us to where we want to be. Having only purpose is like coming up with a bunch of New Year's resolutions and then waiting for the universe to kick into gear and deliver them for you. It's not until we get into action that stuff starts to happen.

DRIVER 2: MAKING PROGRESS

It's key, then, that the second driver for change is making progress. One of the unhealthiest places people can be is when they are feeling stuck, and when working with clients in a clinical setting, I witnessed this time and time again. This feeling builds when we believe that tomorrow is going to be exactly the same as today, and that's when despair sets in.

Nothing is more frustrating and demotivating than feeling like you are working hard but not getting anywhere. Perhaps you have a great idea but get too distracted. (Oh look! A sale is on at Pillow Talk. Why, yes, actually we do need one-million thread count sheets to add to our overflowing sheet cupboard; that's exactly what's missing from my life.) So distracted that we don't deliver on the big stuff. So screw the sheets. Break it down and start getting some forward momentum.

Progress also sits on a continuum (see figure 1.2, overleaf). At the higher end of the continuum is where there's 'no wear' — as in, no wear and tear. This is when you put in effort and it repays you back tenfold. It's those times when the work seems frictionless, you have the right conversations with the right person and things just fall into place.

Down the other end of the continuum is where we're going 'nowhere'. It might be that we've got a mountain of great ideas — maybe we've even got some really, really cool plans — but we just haven't got round to even starting on these ideas because life is so busy. Or we are putting in the effort, but it just feels like we're hitting roadblock after roadblock. That's just like something else coming up and getting in the way, and we feel like we're stuck in that space.

NOWHERE ——————— **NO WEAR**

Figure 1.2: progress continuum

Once again, while progress is critical, without a sense of purpose progress on its own is a bit like watching *The Bachelor* — there's a whole lot of activity and drama but no real point.

Magic happens when we combine the two — purpose *and* progress.

So in those quiet moments when you just wish you had your shit together, rather than reach for more productivity, seek to produce — to bring something into being that didn't exist before. And when you do seek to produce, look at it through the lens of the two drivers for change: purpose and progress. Because when we are clear about purpose, and we are moving forward, we unleash full boss-mode on busy and put it in its place.

In the next chapter, we'll explore how these two drivers interact and the four states we can find ourselves in when they do.

CHAPTER 2
Know your state

Purpose and progress are the critical components required to transition out of overwhelm. But when we look at these components in closer detail, it's how purpose and progress interact that becomes really interesting.

First, have a look at figure 2.1, which shows the first of the four states of the Stand Out Model™.

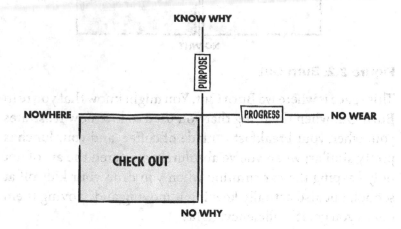

Figure 2.1: Check Out

If you're down in the bottom left quadrant, you're not making any progress at all and have no connection to why. This is where we Check Out. You may recognise this state if you find yourself on Monday morning literally counting down the seconds until Friday afternoon, or if you spend more time on your smart phone than actually being smart.

Often what happens in this state, though, is that we get into action in order to move forward and feel like we're making progress. We shift over to the bottom right side of the quadrant (see figure 2.2), where we're absolutely making progress, kicking goals, winning awards and being recognised by other people as doing amazing stuff—but somehow we've kind of disconnected from why we started all this progress in the first place.

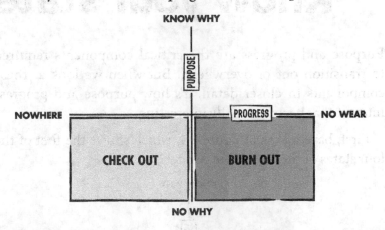

Figure 2.2: Burn Out

This space is where we Burn Out. You might know that you're in Burn Out when the thing that you used to love now frustrates you; when your breakfast is made of coffee, and your lunch is pretty similar; when you've absolutely mastered the art of not only keeping the car running when you drop your kids off at school, but also actually keeping it moving and shoving them out as you go. It's efficiency, right?

Shifting up to the top left quadrant (see figure 2.3) is where we are connected to our purpose, what we want to do and why we want to do it, but we're not feeling like we've got a sense of progress. This is where we Freak Out, because we feel like we have to let go of who we are in order to get moving. We start to even doubt ourselves in this space. We get scared of telling our friends what we want to do, because they've heard it so many times that they're going, 'Really?? I'm not seeing anything happening from here'. Part of our frustration is we feel like we have to let go or lose part of ourselves in order to achieve success.

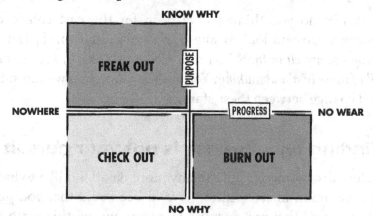

Figure 2.3: Freak Out

The sweet spot is in the top right quadrant (see figure 2.4), when we can get the combination of both purpose and progress. It's in this place that we're connected to why we're doing what we're doing, and we feel like we're making progress — and this is where we completely Stand Out.

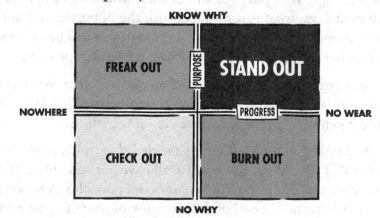

Figure 2.4: Stand Out Model™

19

Standing out isn't about being famous or something you're not. It's about putting aside the expectations, getting clear on your decisions and having a pathway to move towards what matters most. And it's the swagger, self-confidence and assurance of being in that space and standing out.

Where do you think you've been for the past couple of months? Do you look at any of the areas and think, *Hey, I recognise myself in that*? You may well be thinking, *I've been in all of those in about an hour*. You are not alone, and we can shift and change between these states.

Finding one purpose is not your pursuit

Before discussing purpose in any more detail, I'd like to look at a common misconception. We've been sold that you just need to find that one purpose you were put on this earth to do — the one thing you were made for. This pursuit drags us away from exploring an equally important question: how can I find purpose in what I'm doing right here and now?

The thing is, human beings are incredibly adaptable — indeed, our whole existence depends upon it. If you'd been born 50 years ago, your purpose and passion would be completely different from what it is now, because the opportunities and environment would have been different. If you had been born in another country, your purpose would be different again.

Your goal is not about trying to find one thing that you were put on this Earth to do — and you certainly shouldn't feel like until you find this goal you are in a holding pattern.

Best-selling author Jeff Goins tackled this in his book *The Art of Work*. Jeff describes how we all have portfolio lives, and where we are right now is just a part of our portfolio. Whatever you are doing now is part of the evolution of your life. The next part of your portfolio might involve you sailing around the world, or taking up tap-dancing (maybe even both!).

Boredom presents you with the opportunity to reignite in a different direction, or take a deeper dive to another level of mastery. When we see this opportunity as exciting and get curious about 'what next?', we realise that we are in charge of our portfolio.

So your aim is not about just finding one purpose for your life. It's about recognising what is happening in your life right at this point and what's going on for you, and being curious about what parts of this role currently grab your attention. What do you want to dial up even more? Whatever that is, follow that rabbit hole.

What's each state costing you?

Each of the four states comes at a cost — as shown in figure 2.5.

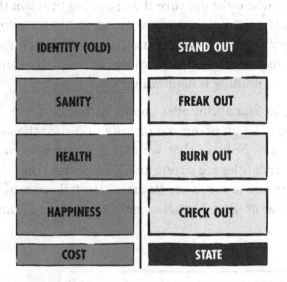

IDENTITY (OLD)	STAND OUT
SANITY	FREAK OUT
HEALTH	BURN OUT
HAPPINESS	CHECK OUT
COST	STATE

Figure 2.5: costs in the four states

When we're in Check Out, the cost is to our *happiness*. We're in Check Out when it's Monday morning at work and we don't just count down the days, we count down the seconds until Friday afternoon; when our best skill is flying under the radar; when we find ourselves sitting on the couch with a bucket of ice-cream watching 20 hours of *Sex in the City* reruns.[1] As we disconnect from what's going on, we start to lose a sense of self, and happiness is the casualty.

The cost to being in Burn Out is to our *health*, because the first three things to go downhill when we're working at a rapid pace are sleep, nutrition and exercise. We burn the candle at both ends, swapping sleep for worry and grabbing the most convenient food options available — and the only sprint we do is to catch the lift. Our sleep, nutrition and exercise drop off despite the fact that these are the three things needed for sustained energy and vitality.

The cost to being in Freak Out is to our *sanity* — not in a clinical sense, but we do start to doubt ourselves. The doubt arises because we're not sure if we're doing the right thing or if we're on the right path, and we question our intuition, which is the very thing that ignites us. The reason we doubt our gut instinct and connection to purpose is because we can't see any progress — nothing is happening.

Being in Stand Out also comes with a cost, and this cost is having to let go of our *old identity*, and shed the skin of the person we've been so that we can embrace who we want to become. Identities are strong and we hold onto them long after they continue to serve us. Perhaps you tell yourself, 'I'm not a runner/writer/musician/leader/_____ (insert your

---

1   Watching 8 hours is perfectly okay and can actually increase your
    happiness, but 10 hours is the tipping point into Check Out.

word)', 'I'm always shy meeting new people', 'I'll never be able to speak in front of people'. The stories we tell ourselves form the identities that we hold onto. Recognising these stories and the identities attached to them, and then letting them go and being brave enough to tell a different story is the cost of being in Stand Out.

When Darren and I started our business we had two very young children and my focus was working on the backend of the business, while Darren presented sessions, delivered keynote speeches and was the face of the company. The backend support had become my identity — until our children reached the ages of four and six, when it was time for me to move into a role of presenting programs and keynotes. I remember getting frustrated at myself for spending so much time fluffing around, and not feeling like I was getting anywhere. I was worrying about the colour and font on my program flyer (irrelevant), rather than actually picking up the phone to talk to clients about what I had to offer (important). One morning I wrote on the whiteboard above my desk, 'Do the work. Be seen'. To now be the person who would 'be seen' was bloody scary, and to become this person I needed to let go of the identity of being behind the scenes.

For a lot of people, this identity change can be such a scary process that they prefer to stay in any of the other states rather than have the courage to let go of their old identity.

How do you see these costs playing out in your life?

What you need to invest in for each state

While each of the four states comes with a cost, they also involve areas you can invest in that will bring you back to focus. These costs and investments are outlined in figure 2.6 (overleaf).

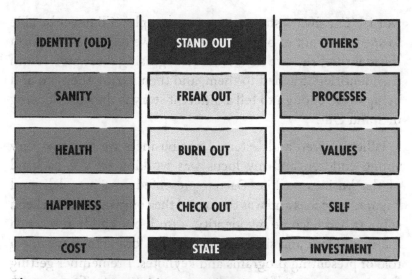

COST	STATE	INVESTMENT
IDENTITY (OLD)	STAND OUT	OTHERS
SANITY	FREAK OUT	PROCESSES
HEALTH	BURN OUT	VALUES
HAPPINESS	CHECK OUT	SELF

Figure 2.6: costs and investments in the four states

Being in Check Out requires individuals to invest in *self* — that is, to come to looking after the mental, physical, psychological, emotional and spiritual parts of self. Recognising that it's not selfish to prioritise our needs but actually necessary to be able to give the best of ourselves to others.

During the state of Burn Out, the focus is on investing in *values*. Values have been shown to make a critical difference within the workplace — from leadership to recruitment to strategic planning. Investing in values is about exploring what is important to you, right here and now.

Discerning between the 'should' and the 'would' are at the heart of this stage. Investing in becoming clearer about what your values are, and in having the language to describe these will mean that other people's expectations don't become a priority. This will give you direction for action.

BEING CLEAR ON WHAT'S IMPORTANT TO US, AND HAVING PROCESSES IN PLACE IN ORDER TO TURN UP, INSPIRE AND GIVE THE BEST TO OTHERS IS KEY TO BEING IN STAND OUT.

Being in Freak Out requires an investment in *processes*. Being connected to purpose is not enough without that action bringing traction — in other words, this is the business end that requires the work to be done. There's nothing sexy about it, it just needs to get done. Get clear on whom you are going to call, sit down and write the chapter of that book, focus on what needs to happen next and put it in a process.

When we're in Stand Out we get to invest in *others*. Often what happens when we're in other states, though, is we spend a lot of time putting others first, and ignoring or putting our needs off. Instead, investing in others requires the building blocks of continually investing in self, values and processes. Investing in others without these building blocks means we don't turn up as our best selves, and we don't give others the best of what's possible. Being clear on what's important to us, and having processes in place in order to turn up, inspire and give the best to others is key to being in Stand Out.

The pursuit of calm (not happiness)

Mountains of books, billions of words published online, and hours of research have been poured into the pursuit of happiness (not to mention the hours Will Smith put into his role in the movie *The Pursuit of Happyness*). And you may be looking to work out of the states of Check Out, Burn Out and Freak Out so you can feel happier.

Research from the likes of Dr Russ Harris and journalist Oliver Burkeman, however, suggests that pursuing happiness is not the goal that most of us desire. In fact, their research suggests that not only is this pursuit draining, but also constant happiness, if we achieved it, is not something we would actually enjoy. This is because experiencing suffering, challenges and frustrations is a key part of what it means to be human.

Rather than happiness, what the modern era is really desperately searching for is the feeling of calm. Not a yoga pose calm, or on top of a mountain, next to a babbling brook of unicorn tears calm, but calm among the chaos.

The person who has the greatest influence is the one who can breathe deep in a crisis. Among the whirlwind of whinging, the juggling of judgements and the catchcries of craziness, what we're really wondering is how we can be that custodian — the one constantly pursuing calm.

So your mission (should you choose to accept it) is to now become the Custodian of Calm — even in a shitstorm. The chaos is not going away. Waiting for a time when the pressure will be off is false hope. You have to find space for calm among the busyness. The actions outlined in the remaining chapters in this book aim to reconnect you back to what's important and offer tips to come back to calm even among the chaos.

Remember: two big things are often missing from our conversations, and we need to skyrocket these to the front:

1. Why this?

2. What's next?

Closing the gap between why and what for those actions that are mission-critical is key to reaching the state of Stand Out. This pursuit comes when we first acknowledge what state we are currently in (Check Out, Burn Out, Freak Out or Stand Out), what being in this state is costing us (happiness, health, sanity or our old identity) and where we now need to invest (in self, values, processes or others).

So, who is the boss wrap up:

You can't change what you don't acknowledge. Be clear on what your roadblocks are.

» Productivity is not the answer. Focus instead on what you are bringing into being, that thing that has your fingerprint on it.

» Fear of criticism is not a reason to stop.

» When we have a strong 'why', purpose drives change.

» Purpose without action, though, is useless — we need to get moving. Progress is the second driver of change.

» Be real about where you are now when it comes to purpose and process, and acknowledge which state has become your default.

» Embrace the mindset of curiosity to explore where you want to be.

» Becoming clear on the costs that accompany each state gives you your motivation for change.

» Calm is your superpower among the busyness. The actions within this book serve to help you in this pursuit.

Part II
Step out of check out

Being in Check Out is the adult equivalent of the child who doesn't want to leave the party but instead of resisting goes completely limp in your arms. This dead weight and passive resistance can be harder to shift than the toddler's temper tantrums. The key when in Check Out is to invest in self, and if this sounds a little like navel-gazing to you (*Come on, Al, you might be thinking, surely you just dust yourself off and get on with the job*), then stick with me. The three actions to focus on to step out of Check Out can be the hardest three to nail.

So let's step into it by exploring over the next three chapters how to hit the reset button, re-establish boundaries, and reconnect with what matters.

CHAPTER 3
Hit the reset button

It's Saturday morning, the sun is shining, the air has a crisp freshness and the clear cloudless sky has not looked this blue in over a week.

But all this goes unnoticed because there's stuff to do. Saturday morning is the time to get ahead, to get on top of things — in between coffee runs, supermarket runs and actual runs. At best, we give the day outside a cursory glance and perhaps say something like, 'Once this is done, I'll get to enjoying that' or 'Next weekend we'll organise a picnic' or 'I'll chill out later when I'm finished' — you know, that mythical, magical time when it will 'all be done', when 'finished' is indeed 'finished'.

Being busy all the time has become a badge of honour — albeit a heavy, awkward, uncomfortable badge that doesn't go with any of your outfits let alone your favourite shoes but, hey, it's the latest fashion accessory and who are you to deny fashion? Dr Brené Brown's research explores this phenomenon, and she claims that in our collective mindset 'exhaustion has become a status symbol'. We're participating in an unspoken race where the most exhausted wins. Think about the conversations you have when people ask you how you are. Your response? 'Busy' [insert overwhelmed sigh, shoulder droop, and eye-roll for effect]. Then the one-upping starts. 'Me too.' 'Yeah? You think you're busy and exhausted?! WELL ... I haven't slept since Ferris Buller had his day off!'[1] This hidden race to tiredness is coming at a physical cost that we often can't see.

Don't get me wrong — I get that sometimes we've got to rip in, work solidly and produce results. Often, as much as these times are full-on, they are also exhilarating — especially when we are on purpose with what we are doing. This is when we are killing it!

The thing is that we then carry this same intensity of action into the everyday, even after the race to productivity is finished. Our fast-paced busyness starts to infect those moments that don't require the same velocity. We worry about slowing down. Like an intense game of Jenga, we fear one wrong move will bring our whole world crashing down. But rather than stop and step away from the game for a moment, we continue running on overload, telling ourselves we'll rest later.

From martyr to warrior

Sitting in Check Out unleashes the inner martyr — that stoic part of us who believes that I've gotta suffer through this because it's just what's gotta be done. The bills need to be paid, the kids need to be fed and, well, this bathroom's not gonna clean itself, so I'd better do it, because if I don't do it no-one will do it, and even when they do it's not good enough anyway, so it's just what's gotta be done and, damn, it will probably need to be done again in two minutes' time, so actually I'm just

---

1   Which was back in the 1980s, peeps. Google it, watch it, then get thee to bed FFS.

gonna live in the bathroom 24/7 so that it's never ever dirty, ever ... *huff*[2]

STEP INTO YOUR INNER WARRIOR.
THE ONE WHO KNOWS THE VALUE OF REST AND
WHO IS CLEAR ON WHAT ACTUALLY MATTERS.

The way to get out of the cycle that martyrdom thinking traps us into is to hit the reset button. The origin of the prefix 're' comes from Latin and means to restore or to return to original condition. Finding ways to hit the reset button for you — that is, actions that leave you feeling refreshed and revived — is the key to investing in SELF.

The ultimate goal here is to move from martyr to warrior. Step into your inner warrior, who knows the value of rest and that recuperation is the key to feeling centred, and who is clear on what actually matters. Let's explore how this works among the busyness.

IT'S TIME TO BE SELFISH

Putting others first is a noble pursuit, and selflessness has an important role in our contribution to the wider community. And it's fraught with danger. Here's why: we're doing it wrong. We're giving to others in a way that diminishes our own needs, and that suppresses what matters to us. This is a recipe for regret and resentment. We end up resenting others for what is being stripped from ourselves. Giving becomes an avenue by which we hope that we're acknowledged, valued and seen as important. If you are a leader within an organisation, your ability to influence is directly proportionate to your ability to look after yourself.

Being switched on to making decisions, being present in conversations, and being able to motivate action is so much

---

2   Transcript of an actual internal rant in my head from last Monday.

easier when you've slept well, eaten what nourishes and looked after your mental wellbeing.

Our society has unique ways of creating the voice inside our head that says it's selfish to focus on ourselves. For example, we hear people say that you can be 'full of yourself'. That we have to prioritise giving the best of ourselves to the people around us and then only after that can we focus on ourselves. The problem is that time never comes.

It's time to be self-kind, self-supporting and self-loving. You don't need to do anything to prove that you are important — by way of simply being here and participating in this life you already are. It's time for us to shake the mountain of judgement and social expectations off the word 'selfish' and realise that turning up refreshed, revived and the best versions of ourselves is the greatest gift we can give to the people around us.

Reset – do it your way

Often when we think about hitting reset we envisage a tropical island, pina coladas, and an afternoon of massages. Ahhhhhhh ... yep, that'll do it. Nice for dreaming but these options don't help us when we're caught in everyday work and life. (The boss seems to have a bit of an issue when you keep bringing Sven and the pina coladas into the weekly team meeting.)

Expanding our definition of hitting reset, we can find multiple ways to feel refreshed and refocused, even on the busiest of days and in the middle of the hardest projects. In fact, the busier the day or the harder the project, the more important it is to carve out pockets of time for reset so you bring your best game back into play.

Knowing what works for you is the key here, because activities that are re-energising will be different for everyone. For some, sitting under a tree reading a book is re-energising;

for others, that sounds like complete torture but lunch and a good laugh with a friend is bliss.

THE RESET THREE-STEP

Whatever activities help you to reset, you need to work through three stages. This process is the key to leveraging every advantage out of these actions.

Step 1: Tune in

Socrates got it right when he offhandedly mentioned one day that to 'know thyself is the beginning of all wisdom'. This step is key to even realising that you are feeling overwhelmed and you need to shake something up. This might sound a bit ridiculous — *like, of course I know when I'm feeling overwhelmed* — but we get caught in just going through the motions and ignoring these triggers (until we absolutely lose it over someone eating too loudly next to us). Self-awareness is critical to realising that you're one step away from this — and that you can actually do something to change your state.

So in order to tune in, ask yourself these questions:

» What are some specific triggers to you feeling overwhelmed?

» How do you behave when you feel out of control? (For example, get huffy, slam doors, make and drink 1000 cups of tea before 10 am.)

» What do you notice in your body when you're feeling overwhelmed? (For example, tight chest, shoulders or jaw, or feeling jittery.)

Step 2: Choose it

Once you're aware that something needs to change, it's time to choose the thing that you could do that will give you the maximum outcome right now. Being aware of the specific actions that work for you — even having a hit list that you can refer to in the chaos — is great planning.

In 'The reset toolbox' section, later in this chapter, I provide a ready reckoner to get you started and give you some options for activities. When you've got yours, write them out on a sticky note and put them at your desk, on your fridge, in the car — anywhere you might need them.

When you choose what activity you'll do, also be aware of the context you are in. These questions will help you get clarity:

» What could I do differently right now?

» What have I got time for now? What can I do later when I've got more time?

» Who else can help with this, or benefit from hitting reset too? (Enlisting a reset buddy is a great way to move your inner-martyr aside.)

Step 3: Do (just) it

I'm sorry, but Nike got it wrong in their 'Just do it' slogan. When it comes to reset, do (just) it. Nothing else. We can undermine even our best efforts to chill out by distracting ourselves and hitting reset with split attention. If you go for a walk but spend your time getting angrier about what Billy said last Tuesday, it's nearly impossible to come back feeling refreshed. Leave Billy at the door before you step out and, if it's something you need to address, pick that issue up again when you step back in — now with a fresher perspective on the situation.

Once you've chosen how you are going to hit reset, drop the guilt and do just that thing. The best way that you can serve and be there for the people around you is to take some time out. The team will be fine if you are not available for an hour, the kids will be okay if you get a babysitter and go to a yoga class, and the spreadsheet won't pout in the corner if you step away from the computer.

Check in with these questions:

» What distractions do I need to drop to focus on resetting?

» Are there any feelings of guilt I need to reframe?

» What difference would having a new perspective make on this situation?

The reset toolbox

As discussed, you have a mountain of ways to hit the reset button, even when you don't feel like you've got time. The following is a toolbox of options to help you hit reset based on the time frame you might have available — right from only having 90 seconds all the way through to that yearly getaway. This is your toolbox of reset strategies you can dip into; add your own and tweak them as you like — but don't wait until the tropical island to hit reset.

Here are some options if you've only got **90 seconds**:

» Take three deep belly breaths.

» Tune into your senses in your immediate environment (name five things you can hear, five you can see, five you can smell, and five you can physically feel).

» Make a 'to-do' list.

» Make a 'have-done' list.

» Practise a quick meditation technique by focusing on breathing in for the count of four and then breathing out for the count of four.

» Focus on an object in the room, count to ten and breathe deeply.

» Decide the next best action to take.

» Create a 'decision gap' (realise you don't have to make a decision right now; allow some time to do this).

» Cease the conversation for 90 seconds, and then go again (go to the loo if you have to).

If you have **10 minutes**:

» Grab a coffee or a tea with a colleague.

» Stand up and stretch.

» Go for a walk.

» Make a herbal tea (make one for someone else too).

» Have an outdoors break (feel the sun on your face and grass between your toes).

» Play your favourite song.

» Dance.

» Phone a good friend for a chinwag.

» Schedule time to talk through what's worrying you with someone.

If you have **30 minutes**:

» Widen the options around what actions you can take.

» Have a debrief with a trusted person.

» Have a walk-and-talk meeting.

» Walk a few blocks or through a local park.

» Connect with someone you trust and talk about how you would like for things to be.

» Write down five things you are grateful for.

» Help someone else.

» Take an express exercise class.

» Have lunch with someone you haven't seen for ages.

For the time you have **after work**, consider these options:

» Exercise (just make sure it's something you actually enjoy, and the more fun the better or else you won't do it).

» Spend quality time with family and friends.

» Grab a picnic and have dinner at the local riverbank or beach, or on a rug in your backyard.

» Do a yoga class.

» Get your art on.

» Organise a holiday.

» Donate your time to a charity.

» Perform a random act of kindness

» Spend time in nature.

Here are some options for your **day of rest or time over a weekend**:

» Sleep and rest (really rest).

» Organise a massage.

» Go on a mini-vacation (an overnight trip).

» Watch your favourite movie.

» Watch a live music show or theatre performance.

» Join in a fun run or other social exercise event (ultimate frisbee anyone?).

» Complete a project at home.

» Visit the local farmers' market.

» Get involved in a local group in your area.

OXYGEN MASKS AREN'T JUST FOR EMERGENCIES

You don't have to go to too many motivational talks before you hear the oxygen mask analogy. If you haven't heard it yet, let me give you the rundown. The bold motivational speaker stands on stage and compares looking after yourself to the safety talk that you get when you are on a flight — you know, that advises that you need to put on your own oxygen mask before assisting others. This then becomes a metaphor that stretches to your personal life, where you need to look after your own needs before taking care of others. The intent behind this metaphor is good — I mean, what good are we to anyone if we don't take care of our physical, emotional and spiritual needs? The problem is that I've been hearing speakers, authors and experts in their field talk about the oxygen mask metaphor for years. And yet all their words haven't changed anything — collectively, the struggle I find is that people are still putting everyone else's needs before their own. Something is not connecting about this metaphor.

This got me thinking: *Why?*

Why, beautiful metaphor as it is, are we still speaking about the goddamn oxygen mask? I was contemplating this when I was on a flight from the Gold Coast to Melbourne. On this occasion, I listened intently to the safety presentation at the start of the flight (rather than switch off, which is what we normally do, right?). And that's when I got the reason this metaphor wasn't sticking. Right there in the safety presentation were the words 'only in an emergency'. The unsaid message in the metaphor was, if you are going to take care of yourself before taking care of anyone else, you'd better have a bloody good reason. The house had better be burning down and it has to be an emergency situation by anyone's standards — not just a little diva, 'Oh, I need more ice in my mojito, stat!' situation.

Because who just grabs an oxygen mask for a normal, non-eventful flight? It's only when the shit hits the fan that we are allowed to make ourselves a priority before snapping into gear to help others. Again the focus is still on how useful we are to other people.

The reality in life, though, is that we need to be reaching for the oxygen mask well before the emergency hits. Taking care of ourselves on the everyday, mundane path that life throws us needs to become our full priority.

TAKING CARE OF OURSELVES ON THE EVERYDAY, MUNDANE PATH THAT LIFE THROWS US NEEDS TO BECOME OUR FULL PRIORITY.

Reset rituals

While the preceding toolbox provides some ideas to get you started in the busyness of the moment, the real key to hitting reset is creating some rituals for yourself that you stick to even if you aren't feeling completely snowed in. These are your self-care rituals that need to become your non-negotiables.

In the following lists I've provided some suggestions for weekly, monthly and yearly reset rituals.

For your weekly rituals, consider:

» lunch with a colleague, friend or your team

» a yoga, Pilates or meditation class

» dinner with the family

» a walk along the beach, river or lake in your area (there's something magical about being in or near water).

And here are some possible monthly rituals:

» Book a massage.

» Have a pedicure or manicure (yep, you boys too).

» Go on a hiking trip.

» Be a tourist at home, using a list of local sites, cafes and restaurants you want to explore.

Yearly could include the following:

» Go on an adventure holiday.

» Visit a health retreat.

» Have a favourite book that you read every year.

» Go on a weekend away with the same people at a similar time each year.

BEWARE THE FALSE BREAKS

When it comes to unpacking the actions and activities that fall under your reset button, be mindful of the false breaks. For example, one of the ways that we can 'chill' is by watching TV. Sure this is a time to switch off your thinking, but it's not always an activity that will leave you feeling refreshed. In fact, TV shows and movies are written and programmed specifically to ignite emotional responses and so harness into your cortisol and adrenaline hormones. While we love these responses, the experience is also exhausting.

One of the other 'false' breaks we can find ourselves trapped in is the day 'off' where we end up running around, sorting out paperwork and standing in queues for hours to get the little stuff of our lives done. Sure these days can feel like progress because we're ticking things off, but they ain't a break. The problem with these false breaks is we delude ourselves into thinking we've unplugged — but then when we get back on the treadmill we wonder why we're already counting down the seconds till our next day 'off'.

BE PURPOSEFUL ABOUT PAUSING

The busier you need to be during the week, the more important it is to carve out moments of downtime now. Don't delay them till later. Be purposeful about pausing, and be realistic about the little moments that help you reset now.

If you sit in the sun and read a book for ten minutes, the balls you've been juggling won't come crashing down. If you have a nanna nap on a Saturday arvo, no-one's going to talk about you (or if they do it will only be out of jealousy). Just remember that it's not the person with the most leave entitlement who wins. Stop waiting till later to address overwhelm. So breathe, carve out space and relax with the same ferocity you work. Your body, your productivity and your peeps will appreciate it more if you stop delaying the downtimes.

In order to do this well, though, we need to be able to set clear boundaries and re-establish them regularly — luckily enough, that's the topic of the next chapter.

Life hack: Disrupt the pattern

Sometimes the patterns (or habits) we fall into can hinder all our efforts to reset. Here's a life hack to break those unhelpful patterns.

The idea

Human beings are pattern-seeking creatures, and sometimes we don't even realise the patterns we fall into. Certain patterns are part of your morning routine,

(continued)

Life hack: Disrupt the Pattern *(cont'd)*

how you make your cup of tea, and the way that you drive home from the shops. In the midst of chaos we crave patterns to fall back on and yet, at the same time, the very patterns we seek can become monotonous and mundane, particularly when we're sitting in Check Out. This life hack is about getting out of your own pattern and changing the channel. You don't have to change the pattern forever, and the change doesn't even have to be particularly grand — it should just shake things up.

The action

Here's how to get out of a monotonous pattern:

1. Choose one aspect of your life (home, work, ballet-lessons, how you make your tea). Just go with the first thing that comes to mind.

2. Come up with one way you can shift the pattern of how you operate in that area (for example, take the stairs not the lift, go to a new cafe, have dinner on the grass outside, kick a ball at the park on the way home, have a stand-up meeting, say good morning in French).

3. Do it.

4. Repeat steps 1 to 3 weekly.

CHAPTER 4
Re-establish boundaries

Feeling resentful; frustrated; like you're being taken advantage of, walked over and uncared for: these reactions are all a result of either poor boundaries or, worse still, no boundaries at all. Sitting in Check Out, we lose sight of ourselves, of what matters, and spend quality time wallowing in self-pity and regret. The cloak of victimhood fits like an old worn shoe that we slip back into time and time again — unfashionable, slightly musty but familiar.

The result is brutal.

We can feel and act like a victim; like our needs don't matter. Our belief that the sacrifice is honourable and others will notice (eventually) is the hope that we don't dare whisper, let alone speak too loudly. When you've tried to stop being the victim in the past, perhaps you've recognised the need to set boundaries, and you may even have gone down the path of speaking up, but these actions didn't stick — which makes the pain dig even deeper. No wonder the cost of sitting in Check Out is our happiness!

From victim to validated

The rise of resentment also occurs when we're stuck in the legacy of past-boundaries — ones that haven't been readjusted despite circumstances changing. You started staying back a little later during the week of your induction so you could feel on top of things in your new role — and seven years later this has become your norm. If what is set in place is not serving you right now, something needs to change. After hitting the reset button (refer to the previous chapter), now is the time to reassess where your time and energy go. Because the truth is, if you don't set your boundaries, others will set them for you.

To set boundaries that stick you need to enlist the help of two qualities:

1. *courage:* to set boundaries around the things that are important to you

2. *conviction:* to turn them into boundaries that stick.

Imagine not feeling resentment when you say yes (and not saying yes through gritted teeth, knowing full well that you'd rather poke your eye with a burnt stick repeatedly ... for hours ... while listening to the next-door teenager's drumming practice than actually do this thing you've agreed to). When we combine courage and conviction we step into being validated.

Shifting from victim to validated starts with giving ourselves permission to say what riles us — and recognising that listening to these objections is important. That your needs matter. It's completely valid to need to have some time and space for yourself, just as it's completely valid to say 'no' to your son's Year 3 reading group, to let your boss know you're not available to work next weekend, and to turn down a great opportunity because it clashes with something you already have on. So start with giving yourself permission to own your truth.

Be warned: it's not easy work setting boundaries, particularly new boundaries. The rewards, however, are worth it. This is your time to move from feeling like the victim to feeling validated; have the courage to listen to your inner voice first, and then have the conviction to follow through.

The three myths about boundaries

Why is setting boundaries so important? Let's answer that question by looking at what our inner gremlins whisper to us about boundaries. These are the three myths about boundaries that need to be pulled down a peg or two.

MYTH #1: BOUNDARIES ARE SELFISH

Society sees being selfish as the equivalent of wearing a blue singlet and short-shorts to a royal wedding. It's basically social suicide and should be avoided at all times. And then our inner monologue kicks into gear with its greatest argument of all time about why not to set boundaries: 'If I set a boundary then it's all about me, and seriously who am I anyway?' This myth trips us up and shuts down our needs in a heartbeat.

TRUTH #1: BOUNDARIES ALLOW US TO CARE MORE DEEPLY FOR OTHERS

Your boundaries aren't all about you. When you set clear boundaries — that is, when you know yourself well enough to be able to articulate your needs — you present your best self at any situation. In a conversation with a colleague or when connecting with close family or a friend, we get to serve and be present for them in a way that we can't be if we are feeling resentful and unheard. Setting boundaries is one of the most selfless things we can do because we get ourselves out of the way and we get resentment off the table. When we sit and wallow in resentment we drive a wedge between our relationships, and the unspoken frustration creates disconnection. Let's go for less 'huffing' and more 'hugging'.[1]

MYTH #2: SETTING BOUNDARIES PUSHES PEOPLE AWAY

This is an interesting myth. Worrying about how the other person involved will react and take our needs stops us from expressing them. 'Well, no I can't,' we tell ourselves, 'because *xx* will take it badly. And I still want them around; I actually still want them in my life'.

TRUTH #2: SETTING BOUNDARIES GIVES OTHERS PERMISSION TO DO THE SAME

The people who are the most compassionate in our world have strong boundaries in their relationships, according to Dr Brené Brown's research. They know exactly what's important to them and they're willing to say no or yes and stand by their conviction because of self-compassion. This doesn't strip them of compassion for others.

When we see others set boundaries and remain compassionate for others, it gives us permission to do the same. For example, in our business we've had a few moments where we've been taken aback by how others operate in business. Not because it was bad or sinister, but because our reaction was 'Are you allowed to do that?' The first time we turned down a potential client because the values of their organisation didn't match with ours, for example, was difficult. I mean, who turns down work? But we had the courage and conviction to do it because we'd seen others do the same.

It turned out that, yes, we were allowed to do that.

---

1   Okay, guaranteeing that might be a stretch but it's possible.

MYTH #3: SETTING BOUNDARIES TAKES TOO MUCH TIME

'Arghhh ... I'd have to sit down and explain this to 50 million people; I don't have the time for that and, really, what's the friggin point? I've got too much on my plate at the moment, and I don't have time for the angst and backlash too'. I hear you, and I challenge you with the following truth.

TRUTH #3: TAKING TIME NOW WILL FREE UP TIME (AND YOUR ANGST) LATER

The top cost of not setting boundaries is time, because being stuck as the victim consumes your thoughts and your mental energy. This is time and space that could be used much more constructively. We teach people how to treat us, so if something or someone is frustrating you and you don't call that out for what it is, you're allowing it to continue, and basically saying that's okay. If someone's actions are frustrating you, it's not about that person; it's about what you haven't put into place — that is, the lack of boundaries that allows this to continue to be okay.

Listen to the niggles

How do you know which boundaries are important for you to set? We can often fall into the trap of hearing someone else's great idea and then taking it for our own. Of course, I'm not against borrowing ideas, but just because something works for Mary-down-the-road doesn't mean it's what we need right now.

When we don't set clear boundaries, it becomes okay for us to blame others and also give ourselves leeway around what really matters. 'Oh,' we might say, 'it's not really that important'. We start to doubt a boundary was ever important, assuming that if it was we would have done something about it. The truth is we didn't fail to set the boundary because it wasn't important, but because we feared the push back that might have come from that tough conversation.

So the way to know which boundaries to focus on is to first listen to your niggles. What are those things that grate on you and aggravate you? Your frustrations can become your guide to re-establishing your boundaries.

The little niggles turn into big frustrations if we ignore them, so they need your attention. Ask the niggle what it's telling you and what it wants, and think about how this could be different for you.

Four tools to set boundaries that stick

Let's unpack four great tools to help you set boundaries that everyone can see.

TOOL #1: EXPAND YOUR OPTIONS; KNOW YOUR PREFERENCES

Often we think in a binary way, believing that our choice is either we do it or we don't do it; it's A or B, yes or no. It's time to lift our head above the dual options to see the whole spectrum of options that are actually available.

If you find yourself in the trap of two options, dig a little deeper. For example, rather than considering 'should I go to this meeting or not?' get your creative on and consider other options. You could:

» go to the meeting and take control of the agenda (avoiding waffle)

» go to the meeting for a short period of time (just the bit you need to influence)

» not go to the meeting but follow up by getting the notes

» not go to the meeting and give a colleague the issues you want addressed or questions to be discussed

» phone into the meeting and be available on speaker phone for discussion, avoiding the downtime of travel, parking and finding the room

» have the meeting at your favourite cafe/restaurant/on a tropical island resort (geez, you'll be busting to go then!).

Starting to explore these options moves the decision away from a simple yes or no answer, and into considering what's most important and how it can be delivered. Through this process you'll get clearer on what your preference is. Understanding what's bugging you, what frustrates you and where that resentment comes from will help you get clearer on what your non-negotiables are.

Whenever you feel stuck on the 'should I or shouldn't I?' seesaw, grab your pen and paper and jot down every option that comes to mind. The wilder the better—don't filter, and just get those little brain bursts down. Even allow yourself to write down exactly how you would like things to play out. What's your ideal? Then consider the gold in even the wildest of answers, and consider the compromise in your ideal. If a tropical island resort is not a feasible option for your weekly team meetings, maybe you could be the cool one who brings leis and coconut oil to the table!

UNDERSTANDING WHAT'S BUGGING YOU, WHAT FRUSTRATES YOU AND WHERE THAT RESENTMENT COMES FROM WILL HELP YOU GET CLEARER ON WHAT YOUR NON-NEGOTIABLES ARE.

TOOL #2: DROP THE 'HINT'

When we know what we want (our preferences) and how it could potentially play out[2] (our options), the next step is to be truly honest with yourself about where the flex level is. Think about

---

2   Insert Hawaiian music and pina coladas.

a rubber band for this metaphor — how far are you willing to flex? And where is your outer stretch point? (Hopefully this is before you get anywhere near your breaking point.) Unless we do the work on understanding and articulating these limits for ourselves, we can't expect anyone else to honour them for us. So often our boundaries are ignored and trodden on because we simply hint at them, rather than being clear on their importance. Or we go the other way and everything is urgent and important and no-one's listening because there's a little bit of 'boy who cried wolf' playing out.

Mind-reading is not a default setting for us human beings. (Of all the amazing things human beings can do, mind-reading is certainly not one of them.) So stop gushing and hoping people will pick up what you're puttin' down. They're dealing with their own stuff and their own internal dialogue, and worrying about who's going to win *The X Factor* next week. Stop assuming they know what you need — they only know when you tell them. So be explicit about what's okay and what's really not okay. Ever. At. All.

So often we fume and 'hint' but don't have the courage to get explicit. I recall running a program where one of the participants started talking about the frustration she felt that every single night after dinner her kids and husband would walk away from the table and leave her to clean up. Her husband would sit in front of the TV and the kids would move on to making a mess in their rooms. Our conversation at the program went a bit like this:

> Her: I've been putting up with this and haven't said anything because I don't want to be the nagging wife, but it really frustrates me.
>
> Me: Have you asked them to help?
>
> Her: Well, I hint.
>
> Me: I'm wondering if you throw the cutlery in the sink sometimes? I know, because I've been there.

Her: Yep, totally.

Me: Does your husband respond to that?

Her: Nope, he just keeps watching TV. He just turns up the volume a bit more.

Any of this sound familiar? Sometimes you need to be bold enough to say, 'Hey, I need this to change. We need to do things differently. What are we going to do about it?' Whatever the outcome is, we can't even start the conversation until we sit down and say, 'I'm not going to put up with this'. For the woman at my program, she needed to say she wasn't going to put up with being the only person to clean up after dinner.

A useful context to also consider when you're speaking up is the required intensity level. Marsha Linehan's work within clinical psychology settings provides an excellent framework to refer to when deciding whether a hint will do or whether the foot has to come down. Linehan identifies that when it comes to setting boundaries, they usually fall into one of two categories: either we're asking for something, or we're refusing something. Adapting Linehan's work, the following frameworks provide a scale from one to five to help you identify your required intensity level in each of the two categories.

Here's the scale for when you're *asking for* something:

1 It'd be kinda nice, maybe, if it's not too much trouble if you did this (but I don't want to impose on you).

2 I'd really like it if ...

3 Let's do this if it works for you ...

4 I need this to happen this way, but I can negotiate on how.

5 Absolutely non-negotiable; this HAS to happen.

And here's the scale for when you're *refusing* something:

1 Hmmmm ... I guess so.

2 Not that keen, really, but I'll do it anyway (half-heartedly).

3 I'm really not keen but I can do it this once.

4 No, I can't do this, but I can compromise on ...

5 THE FOOT IS DOWN![3]

Looking back at the woman from my program who talked about not being the only person to clean up after dinner, her intensity level when she spoke out needed to shift from a one up to at least a four.

Refer to these scales and match the required intensity level to the situation. Have the courage to elevate your request or your refusal if what you're currently doing is not getting traction. Be mindful, though, if everything is at an intensity level of five all the time — doing so won't have as much impact as using this level for the stuff that really matters. Know where your flex is and where your outer stretch point is. Drop the 'hint' and make it explicit. This work is hard — it requires your courage — but it's not as hard as carrying resentment around.

TOOL #3: BE OKAY WITH PUSH BACK

The truth is that we teach people how to treat us. If something is frustrating you and leaving you feeling resentful, it's often because you haven't pulled it up or called it out. The first harsh truth with this tool starts with realising that you are 100 per cent responsible for your role in the situation. Ask yourself this: what have I done or what have I not yet done to make this situation okay?

---

3 *Inside Out* reference. Even if you don't have kids, this is one of Pixar's magic movies with many layers that are relevant for everyone. Watch it and realise you also have a button in you where you can put THE FOOT DOWN!

One of the reasons we don't stand behind the boundaries we want to set is because of the tyranny of 'being liked'. Each and every one of us wants to be liked, and it's not pleasant being the brunt of someone else's frustration. Faced with this dilemma, our ego steps in and says, 'Whoooaa. Hold up there, buddy. I should be liked, I'm a good person, I'm not nasty or mean'.

Instead of worrying about being liked, be anchored in yourself and certain in your worth, and aware that push back doesn't mean that you are a 'bad' person. It means you're a 'boundaried' person. If others don't get that right here and now, they may get it down the track. And that's okay.

The second reality that can hit you smack in the face is that while you've shifted the people around you, you may not — and they may not — like that you've done so. Collectively we crave certainty, and setting boundaries changes the game. Others may riot and revolt in a big way. Push back is not an indication that the boundary is wrong; it's an indication that it's important.

When we have the courage to make a change, for a period of time others need to get up to speed. We need to be okay with the other person saying, 'Hey, I'm not okay with this because it changes the dynamic of our relationship'. Of course, there's every chance they won't articulate it exactly like this, if they articulate their feelings at all. In fact, how this more often plays out is by them ignoring your calls, getting into a huff and sniping at you — but, essentially them not being okay is what they are letting you know.

Push back is also a form of testing your conviction on the boundary. Did you really mean that? Or was that just a Monday whim that won't even last the distance till Tuesday? This is the opportunity to use your grown-up important voice and say, 'Hey, I'm really serious about this'. This is the opportunity to call others' behaviour into line if your boundary doesn't happen, saying something like, 'Look, we had a conversation about *xx*; it hasn't happened, so let's make sure it happens next time'. Sticking to your boundaries sets up the possibility of a really healthy conversation about why and what the new lay of the land looks like for everyone.

The positive flip of the push back is that it may be constructive. Maybe you hadn't considered certain things, or some evidence and data emerges that you didn't have that might change where your boundary starts and finishes. This could be a way for you to continue to grow and make that boundary flexible. Check in with this and see what's constructive — and what's the kind of riot that's really just about someone throwing their toys out of the cot.

TOOL #4: STOP APOLOGISING (#SORRYNOTSORRY)

Why is it when we're given a wrong order at a restaurant or our chicken is undercooked that we start the conversation with the wait staff by apologising? Saying sorry has become a reflex we don't even realise we're doing — it just happens. When it comes to gender, two studies from the University of Waterloo found that while men are just as willing as women to apologise, they had a higher threshold for what they felt they needed to apologise for. Women are much more likely to default to saying sorry over little things.

The language you use when setting boundaries matters. Notice how your language can either allow you to own them or undermine them. A strong boundary is undermined by an apology, and 'sorry' is not the only word that indicates this.

Ellen Petry Leanse, former Google executive, published an article in *Business Insider* after she made a shocking discovery about how often people in the organisation she'd just started working in used the word 'just' in emails.[4] This proportion was significantly higher among women in the organisation. Maybe you use something similar to the following:

'I just wanted to check in ...'

'This will just take a moment ...'

'If you could just give me an answer ...'

'I just wanted to follow up ...'

'Just seeing if that makes sense ...'

Leanse believes that the sample from her organisation is a reflection of a far greater endemic across our society. The use of 'just' is not all about being polite, in a subtle way it's a permission word — an apology for interrupting, a quiet voice that says 'don't mind me'. When we remove the j-word from our language, written and verbal, we have greater confidence and what we say holds greater weight. The phenomenon of 'oh, sorry' is alive and kicking in our language and needs to be kicked to the curb.

Set it — the universe will test it

In the very moment that we set a clear boundary, it's my experience, and possibly yours, that the universe conspires to test our conviction. Even on the little things.

Imagine setting the boundary to leave work at 5 pm every afternoon rather than slipping into working late. You set this so you can spend more quality time with your kids/partner/pet/yoga instructor before the night rush happens. Invariably, the very next afternoon at 4:55 pm you receive a critical email or a phone call that requires something urgent to be done right now — that thing that only you can do (or so you believe). What do you do?

---

4   Explore the article here: www.businessinsider.com/former-google-exec-says-this-word-can-damage-your-credibility-2015-6

The curse of 'just this once' kicks in, and you hang around till 5:30 pm promising your kids/partner/pet/yoga instructor that you'll make it up to them tomorrow — only to have it happen again, and again. Setting the boundary at leaving at 5 pm, and then letting it become more like 5:15 pm or 5:30 pm for the next week undermines what you've put in place — and people are going to listen to what you do more than what you say.

Regardless of how minute or major the situation is, establishing and re-establishing boundaries starts with you. Having conviction around your boundaries, particularly around the little things, gives others permission to do the same.

> **REGARDLESS OF HOW MINUTE OR MAJOR THE SITUATION IS, ESTABLISHING AND RE-ESTABLISHING BOUNDARIES STARTS WITH YOU.**

Through the busyness, personal boundaries can be the collateral damage that leaves us feeling resentful, even guilty, because we haven't shown the best of ourselves.

In the everyday moments

Setting (and resetting) your boundaries happens in the small, everyday moments. It's picking up a call from someone and making it clear from the start how much time you've got to give this conversation. It's me answering a call from my EA[5] and saying, 'Hey Trace, I've got five minutes, so shoot'. I don't have any other agenda, what I'm saying is not code for 'you're

---

5   The greatest EA on Earth, mind you. And, no, you can't steal her. Ever. If you do, I'll hunt you down.

wasting my time', or 'you've rung me too much today'; it means nothing more than exactly what it is.

In order to set boundaries that stick, we need to first have the courage to admit them to ourselves, and then the courage to speak them and the courage to back them. We need to have the conviction to admit what we need, deflect it, and the conviction to live it. So step out of victim mentality and embrace the validation that you are worth it. When you do you're more compassionate and present to others. And when you own your boundaries, you give others the permission to own their boundaries too. And you can focus on reconnecting with what matters.

IN ORDER TO SET BOUNDARIES THAT STICK, WE NEED TO FIRST HAVE THE COURAGE TO ADMIT THEM TO OURSELVES, AND THEN THE COURAGE TO SPEAK THEM AND THE COURAGE TO BACK THEM

Life hack: Frustration rant

This life hack gives you a process to blurt out frustrations, even rant about them, and then shift into action.

The idea

Frustrations grow and fester until we give them air. Often options are completely hidden from us until we bounce our frustrations off a trusted friend. But without a good process, the ranting can go on and on and on and nothing's been solved. However, you often know what you need to do if you can see beyond the rant. This is your process to do that.

(continued)

Life hack: Frustration rant (cont'd)

The action

Here's how to move from frustration to action:

1. Grab a trusted colleague/friend/DJ/the local barista and ask them for some of their valuable time.

2. For five minutes (and five minutes ONLY), go on your rant.

3. When your five minutes is up, briefly identify what's outside your control.

4. Identify what's inside your control.

5. Decide on the next thing you are going to do.

Your colleague/friend/DJ/local barista really doesn't have to do much more than keep you on track with these questions, nod occasionally and be a sounding board.

CHAPTER 5

Reconnect with what matters

When projects stretch out longer than anyone had ever anticipated, when the hurdles you face turn into six-foot-high double-glazed impenetrable windows — this is when our resolve is truly tested. The promises you'd made to yourself that you'd eat better, exercise more and look after yourself better get washed away in an instant by a bottle of red wine and an almond Magnum ice-cream. These are the types of moments when cynicism clouds our usually optimistic approach.

Nope. I won't let that one slide, actually. Let's get real. Cynicism doesn't just cloud; it takes over like an infectious disease. Nothing is immune when cynicism turns up. Even Great-Grandma's heirloom vase that has held a sacred place in your family for years is seen as a 'dust-gathering, useless waste of crappy-glass' if you've got a cynical view happening.

I call this the 'c-world'. And trust me, this c-world is far more destructive than the other c-word. Cynicism is ruthless and nothing is off limits when it shows up. It feeds on itself quicker than a tropical tornado at sea.

All of us dabble in cynicism, but a few of us are experts, wallowing in it up to our eyeballs. The more disconnected we feel from our purpose, and the more that we feel like nothing we do is making progress, the more likely it is that cynicism will be what shoots out when we open our mouths or type an email. 'What's the point ...', 'it'll never work ...', 'tried it before ...', 'why even bother ...', 'Marjorie and her homemade cupcakes! Damn uppity 83 year olds'. Cynicism. At its best.

Salvatore Maddi, personality researcher at the University of California, suggests that the buds of the cynical flower are formed when people put in an effort to achieve a target — like starting a new business venture, or asking someone out on a first date — and their efforts are unsuccessful. The gap between what they expected, even hoped for, and reality leaves individuals feeling helpless and with a sense that their efforts don't really matter. The prevalence of cynicism in Check Out is, therefore, expected — but it doesn't have to be tolerated.

Rather than welcome cynicism in, make up a bed for it in the spare room and invite it to stay until Christmas; your goal is to create an environment where cynicism feels really uncomfortable and awkward, so that it eventually decides to find somewhere else it can flourish. Even after we've hit the reset button and re-established our boundaries, we can still be faced with the all-consuming wash of 'but really what's the point?' This means the third action required to step out of Check Out is to reconnect with what matters.

From cynical to grateful

The opposite end of the cynicism continuum is gratitude. It's impossible to be cynical and grateful at the same time — they're mutually exclusive states. When we're truly grateful — when we're thankful for what we have in our lives and what matters to us — we are able to combat the belief that nothing will ever change. Gratitude is the secret antidote to every ailment that manifests itself from cynicism.

Gratitude is derived from the Latin root 'gratia', meaning 'grace', and the idea of receiving something for nothing. Within psychology, gratitude has been pegged as the 'healthiest' emotion we can experience, with benefits in everything such as improved self-esteem, better relationships, positive impacts on our physical health, improved sleep and greater happiness. Despite these benefits, what the research also shows is that while gratitude is super-easy when we're feeling great, when we're up to our eyeballs in cynicism, gratitude can be the last thing we feel like indulging in. In fact, even the idea of someone mentioning the idea of gratitude can bring on a cynical rant, along the lines of 'Seriously? Are you friggin kidding me now?', 'You just don't get what I'm facing', 'There's nothing that can shift this' and 'I'll be damned if Majorie didn't drop those delicious morsels around just to spite me'.

If you've experienced trouble feeling grateful of late, the key is to shift from self-harm to self-calm, accept what is, and reconnect to what you are awesome at. Let's explore these in more detail.

Self-harm versus self-calm

Our inner voice can be a persuasive bugger. Persistent. Consistent. Insistent. (These are what I call our 'three tents'. See what I did there?[1])

This inner voice thingo — she's a belligerent one. And these three tents show up even in spite of evidence to the contrary. If you don't believe me, think about what you do in the face of a compliment from others. If anything like most people, your knee-jerk reaction is to dismiss it instantly. 'Oh, I'm not as good as ...', 'That was nothing ...', 'Yeah, but you should see

---

1   Yep, they all end in 'tent'. Genius.

how much I suck at …'. Compliment dodged and deflected. Opportunity to connect with what you are good at … gone.

Away from others, this inner voice can be even more harmful. You forget a friend's birthday and you are the worst person in the world; you get a speeding fine and you should march in to hand over your licence (seriously — who ever let you drive?). You trip over a stick on the pavement and you should completely give up walking — for life. Ouch, ouch, ouch. Self-harm always starts in your head, and if you let it run asunder, something much worse happens. We shift into self-harm behaviours.

Self-harm behaviour shows up in the actions we engage in. We sit on the couch inhaling a tub of ice-cream, we go on a spending spree and max out the credit card when our capacity to repay it is reduced, or we push ourselves harder than our bodies can endure in an exercise session and end up injured for a few weeks. We've all been there: things aren't going that great, life deals us a crappy hand and what do we do? We double-dose it with self-harm talk and behaviours to dig into the sore even deeper. This internal self-harm exacerbates our worst fears and keeps us in a mindset of cynicism. But I'm here to tell you: the c-world sucks for a visit and positively blows to live in permanently.

From a physiological perspective, when we are in self-harm our bodies respond through our sympathetic nervous system — one of two systems that work under the autonomic nervous system and so regulate the unconscious functions in the body. The sympathetic nervous system is responsible for our body's 'fight, flight or fright' response, so when it kicks into gear we are alert to our environment and ready to respond. Our adrenaline is pumping and then cortisol kicks in for good measure. This concoction leaves us feeling 'on edge' and while this is actually an ancient defence mechanism, when this response becomes chronic it can impact our bodies in various ways, including an increased risk of heart conditions, weight gain, reduced immunity and ongoing fatigue. All this creates a fertile environment to engage in further self-harm.

The way to counteract this vicious cycle is to shift out of self-harm into self-calm — that is, to find ways to change both our psychological and physiological responses. Let's start with the physical stuff, and then move onto the thinking stuff.

LET'S GET PHYSICAL

No need for leg warmers and shocking 1980s fashion here — it's a bit more 'sciencey' than that. Self-calm requires us to shift from our sympathetic system processes into our parasympathetic system. Our parasympathetic nervous system is the calming response in our bodies, responsible among other things for our 'rest and digest' response, and regulating down both blood pressure and temperature. The parasympathetic response slows our heart rate, conserves energy, and kicks into gear activities that occur when our bodies are in rest, such as effective digestion. From a brain response perspective, our ability to think rationally, make clearer decisions and view a situation through an optimistic perspective is heightened when our parasympathetic response is in control. 'Tis a good place to be if you're in the midst of Check Out, basically.

When we are stepping into self-calm, being conscious of a calming internal dialogue that is filled with compassion helps. But sometimes the fastest way to experience self-calm is to use physical instead of mental methods. Self-calm behaviours can get us out of self-harm's way and allow us to move from cynicism to gratitude, all while giving us loud and clear biofeedback that we are regaining control and clarity. Eat well, sleep sounder and move smart are all ways to move into self-calm. The following table outlines some more.

SELF-HARM ACTIONS	SELF-CALM ACTIONS
Focus on hurrying	Focus on deep breathing
Spend more than you can afford	Spend time with a friend
Drink a whole bottle of wine	Drink 3 to 4 litres of water per day
Stay up late watching crap TV	Rise early and see the sunrise (best TV show ever!)
Consume the Nutella jar	Consume time in nature

You see as you reflect on the preceding list, you might have a voice in your head saying, 'The list on the left sounds divine!' But that's crap, and not sustainable over the long term. It's a c-world voice trying to defend your current behaviours. The list on the right is where Stand Out lives. And no downturn, negative or self-harm is hidden in there — just pure, beautiful self-calm behaviours. So go on … start today. What are some self-calm behaviours you can engage in right now? You head off and take care of that, and I'll be waiting for you when you get back.

Cue daggy elevator music …

Right, you're back! Awesome, because now it's time for a biggie. Let's move on to tackling the greatest self-calming thing you can do: moving into acceptance of your current situation.

ACCEPT WHAT IS

Let's play a game — you know, the game where I say a word and you say the first thing that pops into your head. Such as:

When I say blue you say _____?

When I say sleep you say _____?

When I say coffee you say _____?
(#now #more)

So when I say the word 'accept', what is the first thing that comes to mind? For most people, this word is connected to a sense of 'giving up' — of resignation and feeling like the situation is never going to change. Acceptance seems to some to be the verbal equivalent of throwing your hands in the air in a huff because nothing else can be done. An overriding passivity seems to reside within the word that can rile the defensive activist that lies within us to roar, 'I'm not having a bar of that. I'm not giving up'.

This common social definition of acceptance is inherently a passive one. We can take another view of acceptance, however — one that is known in psychology as 'active acceptance'. This view of acceptance is drawn from the modern psychological therapeutic approach of acceptance and commitment therapy (ACT). This approach originated in the mid 1980s and was different from other approaches at the time because it proposed that, rather than fight against pain, fear and sadness, we could head down an alternate pathway; we could 'sit with it'. Dr Russ Harris is a forerunner in bringing this approach to popularity and making it accessible for many people through his best-selling books and, according to Harris, the objective of ACT is to not eliminate difficult feelings, but to become present to what is happening. The aim is to just 'notice', defuse our sense of self from what is happening and then choose the next steps based on personal values and what's important in this situation.

The reason our knee-jerk reaction is to think of acceptance as passive is because we layer the situation we are facing with judgement. But active acceptance ... ahhh! It truly is wonderful stuff. This acceptance is built on our ability to remove judgement, and to look at what is happening, including our reactions, from a neutral perspective. We can get curious, inquisitive, and even a little scientific about what is happening right here and now. The key is to be able to eyeball reality with the mindset of, 'It's not bad, it's not good, it just is'.

You know those moments when you are in Check Out: when you arrive at work on Monday morning and start counting down the seconds till Friday afternoon, when the highlight of your day is when it finishes, when the grind is up in yer grill and just won't back off. Actively accepting this reality requires you to shake off judgement and repeat, 'It's not bad, it's not good, it just is'. For those times when life throws you curve balls of frustration in rapid-fire, and you feel surrounded by a cluster of idiots who can't seem to think for themselves, repeat to yourself, 'It's not bad, it's not good, it just is'.

Now I know that internal defensive roar is firing up inside of you right now, screaming, 'Are you serious, Ali?!! I can't accept stupidity when it's so obvious these idiots just need to change!' My question to you is how is stewing in the frustration helping you to move forward? Is getting caught up in the 'right fight' really changing the situation for you in the next five minutes? Active acceptance requires you to put all your cards on the table without judgement, including recognising your reaction to what is happening. It's not bad, it's not good, it just is. When we are able to assess those cards on the table without judgement, we have a clearer opportunity to drive change — rather than spend our resources and energy fighting what is happening.

IT'S NOT BAD, IT'S NOT GOOD, IT JUST IS.

And remember: the opposite of acceptance is denial. Imagine after a bountiful Christmas season you go to put on your jeans and find they are tighter than usual. It's not until you accept that you had a few more fruit mince pies than usual (and maybe a few rum balls ... oh and that fifth helping of trifle) that you do anything to change the situation. When you start blaming the dryer for shrinking your jeans, however, or the brand for the poor quality of stretch in the fabric or, worse still, when you beat yourself up for having over-indulged, you're stuck. And all that doesn't help you getting about finding a solution, does it?

DRIVE WHAT COULD BE

When we reach that point psychologically of accepting what is, we now have a platform to drive what could be (see figure 5.1). If you're angry, frustrated or resentful of a situation, the key is not to deny these reactions. Instead, the key is to get curious. (*Oh, that's interesting — what sits behind that?*) This curiosity gives you the fuel to drive change, to explore possibility and get active about changing what's in your control. Possibly the only thing in your control is your reaction to a situation.

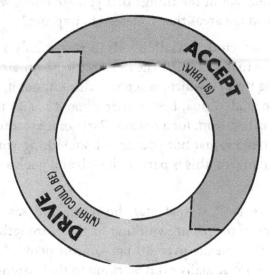

Figure 5.1: accept what is, drive what could be

It's only from the platform of accepting what is that you can then take ownership about what happens next. It's not bad. It's not good. It just is. And how do I want it to be different? What's my next move? Make this your new mantra.

Reconnect to what you are awesome at — your strengths

Marcus Buckingham is a British-American *New York Times* best-selling author and consultant who is on a personal mission to start a strengths revolution. Buckingham's research finds that people get the best results when they are focusing on their strengths, rather than putting all their efforts into improving their weaknesses. While this might sound obvious, the reality is that we (and those around us) spend more time focusing on the things that we're not great at than we do working on the things that we are awesome at. Think about the last performance review that you had at work, and what you remember most about that conversation. Do you remember talking much about the things that you are doing well, or did you dwell on the areas that you need to improve?

What research from Gallup tells us is that only 17 per cent of people actually say that they're working to their strengths most of the time — which, when you think about it, is just not very much at all. Look, I get it that when it comes to work or study, it's called work for a reason. Parts of it are always going to be, you know, just not you or not something you feel like you're thriving in. This is part of the job and you've just got to do it.

When we look at that stat, however, and say that only 17 per cent of people are working to their strengths most of the time, that means over 80 per cent of people are saying that they're not actually even working to their strengths most of the time at work. Imagine how your work life would change if you could show up and give the best of who you are to your team and to your organisation. Or even to the people around you. If you're studying or doing other community work — however you're out connecting with people — imagine if those people got the best of you. Wouldn't that be an absolute game changer?

Further stats from Gallup show people who use their strengths every day are six times more engaged in their jobs, and that they're 38 per cent more productive when working within their strengths. How do you put your strengths to work?

Working inside or outside of your strengths is amplified when we're sitting in Check Out. Even the activities that we usually love can feel like a chore. This is where hitting the reset button is key to reconnecting to who you are and what you are good at. Then taking some time out to uncover your current strengths and bring them to the forefront of your focus is important.

So what are your top five strengths? A number of resources can help you to uncover your strengths in a deeper way.[2] But you may already have the answers. Just taking the time to bring your awareness to this area can also give you some glimpses into what you are awesome at.

Grab a piece of paper and write down those things that your friends and colleagues say that you do really well. Also think about what others come to you for. It might be advice, a task, or information. What things do you do automatically and maybe don't pay too much attention to because they come easily for you?

Before you dive straight into writing down your strengths, also consider your past two weeks and think about the activities you've loved doing, where you've found yourself caught up in the moment. On the flipside, consider the activities that you've loathed doing. What things have you avoided or dragged your heels doing?

Jot down these activities in the following boxes.

---

2   The Gallup Strengths Center (www.gallupstrengthscenter.com) and the StrengthsFinder tool available there are a great starting point.

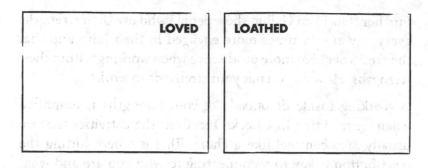

LOVED	LOATHED

Your strengths aren't all about the things that you are good at, because you might have some activities that you can do, and do well, but they just don't light you up. The key to reconnecting with your strengths is to notice if those activities energise you or drain you. Think about the activities that you walk away from absolutely buzzing. These activities might be really challenging — they might even be frustrating when they don't work or a source of stress and pressure — but that's not a sign that they drain you. Again thinking about the past two weeks, write down the activities you did that energised you. What were you doing? Who were you with? What exactly about that task energised you?

Then think about those activities that drained you. They might be activities that you are actually really good out. Maybe they're activities that you are better at than others so others are drawn to actually giving you those activities, because you're really quite good at them. But even when you do them well, you walk away feeling drained — you feel absolutely kind of exhausted from them. For me, I'm pretty good at pushing a vacuum cleaner around the house, I can get into the corners and do a great job, but it drains me. It's not something that I'm lining up to do again and again and again.

Jot down your responses on the activities that energise you, and those that drain you, in the following boxes.

WHAT ENERGISES YOU?	WHAT DRAINS YOU?

Using this data, write down five of your strengths. Blink it, don't think it when it comes to your strengths. Write down the first five things that come to mind — they don't have to be perfect, they don't have to be anything too ground-breaking, just get 'em down. The fact that you rock at playing the harmonica is completely okay to write here — in fact, it's pretty damn awesome because I've tried those things and it ain't pretty.

Write down here five of your strengths, in any order:

1 _____

2 _____

3 _____

4 _____

5 _____

Have you got your list? Great.

The next step is to consider how you can bring your strengths to life. Really, the key goal is matching your strengths to your activities and what you are living. Have a think about where those gaps exist for you. When you look at your list of your top five strengths, are you living them? If not, where are those gaps? Where are the ones that you might want to amplify or do more with? When I filled out the strengths finder questionnaire recently, one of my top five strengths was all around empathy, and this absolutely made sense for me. I kind of went, 'Yeah, that's something that I just do naturally'. But seeing this as one of my strengths made it become really intriguing for me, and I've now been doing a whole heap of research about this area — what is empathy? How do other people look at it, and how can we actually develop it and grow it in our lives and in our places of work? For me, this process was actually a trigger to get into action around living empathy more and honing that skill, even more.

When you look at your top five strengths, is there one that intrigues you? What's the one strength that you want to step up into more, and where you might want to grow, to develop, to hone, to expand? Pick out one strength that is a burning ambition for you, and think about where you are on a scale of one to ten with that strength. You might be sitting at about a seven. With a bit of work, a bit of development and focus, working on that strength may mean you can get yourself to an eight or a nine, where you are absolutely kicking your strides in that strength.

Imagine if you bring the best of who you are to all you do. How much would that be an absolute game changer to the work that you do, the study that you do, and the relationships that you have with the people around you? Don't wait for the perfect time, just get moving now — because I promise you, when we invest time in our strengths, it actually repays us.

IMAGINE IF YOU BRING THE BEST OF WHO YOU ARE TO ALL YOU DO. HOW MUCH WOULD THAT BE AN ABSOLUTE GAME CHANGER TO THE WORK THAT YOU DO, THE STUDY THAT YOU DO, AND THE RELATIONSHIPS THAT YOU HAVE WITH THE PEOPLE AROUND YOU?

It's time to own it (time that is)

Time is the most precious resource we have, and most of us don't feel like we've got enough of it. We continually feel like we're running out of it, and begrudge it when we do. (Seriously, where has this year gone??!!)

And yet, at the same time, every morning you get a fresh new allocation — this is the one thing every person on the planet shares. The most successful people on the planet have exactly the same amount of time as you.

Time.

Is it a scarcity or an abundance?

The truth is it's neither. It just is.

It's our mindset and our actions that skew time into being something we either wrestle with or embrace.

I know I'm ready to stop being surprised by time passing (seriously, it happens every day) and to stop being a slave to it.

So here are three habits to help you stretch time so that you begin to use it to your advantage, rather than being chased down by it:

1. *Stop ... drop and roll:* okay, maybe not those last two. But definitely stop. Stop what you're doing, stop rushing, and stop the inner dialogue. Take a deep breath (or three) and repeat.

2. *Triage like a master:* the problem is not a full calendar, the problem is the pull in too many directions. This is where you need to master all the ruthless triage ninja skills you have and unleash them. Take stock in this moment — what's the most important use of your time right now? Ship what you need to, outsource whatever you can, make swift decisions and move forward.

3. *Steal it:* grabbing that extra coffee on a busy day, sharing a laugh with your buddy on the way back from the tea room, ducking in for a slice of your favourite pie (custard or apple for me) on the way back from lunch. For all these decadent indulgences you make in your day (and you do deserve them), you steal time. And so you should — but be more purposeful about it. Steal time for the things that you love to do. If you love taking photos, grab your camera and sneak away for a quickie (shoot that is), or leave your phone on the desk and step outside to be kissed (sun-kissed, that is). Just make sure you steal time for what makes your heart skip a beat. Stretch and use time to your advantage rather than be constantly chased down by time. Trust me, for the things that simply need to get done, there's enough time to make it happen.

Life hack: Soul-nourishing list

Knowing what nourishes your soul helps you to prioritise these activities in your life.

The idea

Often we are asked to think about goals — you know, what we want to achieve for the future, the New Year's resolution type stuff. While this is good, the process doesn't always reconnect us back to the stuff that matters here and now. We are thinking about a future self, rather than our current needs.

The action

For the next week, write down a list of all the things that nourish your soul. When I did this life hack for the first time, I expected that some of the things usually on my long-term lists would also be on my list here. But what I've found is that, over the week time frame, the little stuff took pole position.

Here are a few of the soul-nourishing things that made the cut for me:

» swimming at the beach

» hanging out with our family of four and sharing a laugh

» watching the sunrise

» using my creativity.

When I realised what nourished my soul, it was obvious that all of these things were well within my control to make time for every week.

So your life hack here is to write down a list of things that nourish your soul. You might be surprised at what makes the cut.

Check out wrap up

Want to move from martyr, victim and cynical to warrior, validated and grateful? Come back to these three key actions:

1. *Hit the reset button:* this can be in the little moments on a busy day, or in the more significant need-to-book-accommodation kind of way. Don't follow what others do; instead, find those things that work for you.

2. *Re-establish your boundaries:* have the courage to tune into those things that niggle you, and have the conviction to say no. Re-establishing boundaries may result in push back from others, but this doesn't diminish your boundaries. It just means your conviction needs to be strengthened.

3. *Reconnect with what matters:* combat cynicism through the gratitude of what is working well. Reconnect with the things that you rock at, and the strengths that you can amplify.

PART III
Combat
burn out

In 1974, Herbert Freudenberger, a German-born American psychologist, noticed something that intrigued him. An increasing number of his patients were presenting with similar conditions of mental and physical exhaustion connected to their professional life. He was the first person to coin the phrase 'burn out' as a way to describe the exhaustion he was witnessing. What Freudenberger saw was that people were experiencing a significant impact on their health and wellbeing connected to the busyness of what consumed their time. For most people, that's work.

Over the past 40-odd years, burn out has become not only an idea to coin but, for many professionals in the Western world, also a way of operating — the new norm. In order to step into Stand Out, we need to focus on strategies to combat being in the state of Burn Out. While our first reaction might be to jump off the treadmill and do less, this step back into inactivity can lead to us slipping back into Check Out. Instead, the way to vitality and health is through values. Knowing the 'why' behind the work and having a clear intent behind your actions begins with defining what's important, and then designing a values-aligned life and defending these values. This process of define, design and defend is covered over the next three chapters.

Let's start by getting clear on what actually matters.

CHAPTER 6
Define what's important

Do you believe the world is getting slower or faster?

Is the world getting more relaxed or more agitated?

Are we getting more certain or more uncertain?

Have I cheered you up yet? Because it's highly likely you've answered similarly to the thousands of people I've asked these questions to — and recognised that the world is getting faster, more agitated and more uncertain. Arghhh. As we've already covered in the introduction to this book, the world is moving at a rapid pace. Change is here to stay and it's not waiting for any of us to catch up and jump on board.

This all leaves us operating in a frantic state — shifting from one busy moment to the next before collapsing into bed. Only to get up the next morning to rinse and repeat.

In our workplaces, the collective impact of busy has a cumulative and contagious effect, because our ability to influence others is more powerful than we take credit for. An experiment done by the Max Planck Institute for Cognitive and Brain Sciences highlighted how contagious stress can be. Observers watching others go through a stressful experience were found to have an increase in cortisol levels. This response was increased when participants were observing someone they knew and cared for. This empathetic response can result in stressed and agitated behaviours when we see others behaving this way — meaning our behaviours are contagious.

The cost of Burn Out

When we are in Burn Out, the cost is to our health. In this quadrant, we can be kicking goals, even smashing targets; but we're doing so at the cost of looking after ourselves. As we run from one project to the next, juggling ever-faster speeding balls, the first three things to drop off our list are sleep, nutrition and exercise. We lose sleep worrying about the sheer amount of stuff we have to get done (and will Brian[1] ever be able to do his job properly — seriously!), we grab food where we can and eat it on the run — fast and nasty is usually the choice — and the most exercise we get is running to catch the elevator to our next meeting. Our focus on these health behaviours goes to the bottom of our pile right at the time when more energy, not less, is required.

On a personal level, the impact of busy, particularly when we've lost sight of 'why' we're busy, occurs across all aspects of our health — and health is not just about going on Weight Watchers and busting out Zumba moves. Eating and exercising well, although important, is still only a limited view of what encapsulates health. I've certainly had times when I've been eating okay and still joining in with my local running group, but the sheer weight of overwhelm leaves me snapping at the kids more than I should. So health covers other aspects of our lives, including relationship health.

Dr Lissa Rankin is an American physician who discovered something interesting when talking with her patients. While

---

1   Sorry, Brian. Not you, the other Brian.

her patients were presenting with a physical ailment, when she asked them, 'What do you need to heal?', the responses were things like, 'I need to change my job', or 'I need to sort out my debt', or even 'I need to leave the relationship I'm in'.[2] These insights prompted Dr Rankin to expand our definition of 'health' to include aspects of our lives that contribute to our overall wellbeing. Dr Rankin's work has identified that the following aspects of our lives have as much impact on our health as what we eat and how we move:

» physical health

» mental health

» relationship health

» financial health

» creativity

» spirituality

» sexuality

» work/life purpose

» physical environment.

As we explore the cost being in Burn Out has to our health, it's important that our definition of health involves these other aspects of our lives. We'll circle back around to some of these aspects as we start to unpack what's important in our lives.

The universal truth

Throughout my career I've been fascinated with understanding how different people respond to the same scenario or situation. For example, why is it that only 20 per cent of soldiers who

---

2   Lissa's TED Talks are essential viewing to get you thinking differently about your health.

endure horrendous atrocities in war situations will experience post-traumatic stress disorder, when 100 per cent of those people have a legitimate reason to experience it? Why is it that of two different teams in the same organisation experiencing the same restructure and unrest of change, one goes into complete meltdown and the other thrives?

Why is it that for some mums, five kids aren't enough? I have a brilliant friend who has three kids of her own, would often look after mine too when they were younger (making it five kids under five), along with ten chickens, two dogs, two guinea pigs and a pet lizard. And she would absolutely thrive for the afternoon. Put me in that situation and I'll be rocking in the corner quicker than you can say 'Put the bubbly on ice'.

The question for me in this area of busyness was where does this sense of overload come from? From my research and work in this space, I can identify one place that this sense of overload comes from. It's the same for every person — you and me — and it's: *you* (and that includes me).

This is one of those pills I found hard to swallow, because what comes to mind is, 'Yeah, but ... you haven't been to my workplace; you haven't met my boss/colleague/spouse/partner/dreaded mother-in-law!'

The thing is, I've worked with people who are facing incredibly tough situations and teams who are driving hard change, and their sense of overload always comes from the same place — how those individuals respond to the situation. One of the few things under our control in the environment of relentless change is how we choose to respond to situations — and we *always* have a choice.

Now, you might be right in your reaction, and you might be right in how you feel. My question is not whether you are right or wrong. My point is, is your reaction serving you? If your reaction to a situation is making you feel more overloaded and stressed, it may not be serving you well at all.

Because the one universal truth is you can't do everything, and you can't please everyone.

Now you may well be thinking to yourself, *Yep, I know that, Alison.* This might even be the same advice you've given to a friend who's busting themselves for their boss and still being reprimanded for not doing it right.

YOU CAN'T DO EVERYTHING, AND YOU CAN'T PLEASE EVERYONE.

While you may 'get' this truth for other people, however, one of the things us professional head mechanics know is that we often think different rules apply to ourselves, and that for some people a little voice inside is saying, 'Bullshit — I can!' And those are the ones who will work late to prove it. They will bust their hump, work back late, take on more than they should and try to get it all done in the hope of pleasing everyone.

But no matter how many hours you put in, no matter how many people you try to please, this universal truth still stands.

You can't do everything, and you can't please everyone.

This might sound a bit defeatist and even negative. But 'getting' this, understanding that we can't do it all, is one of the most liberating realisations we can have. Because now we get to choose what we do, and we get to choose who we want to influence the most — and the lens to making these choices are your values.

Your values – from obscure to clear

Values are a concept that has been studied and explored in great detail, with various definitions. Over the past decade I have worked closely with executives, teams and organisations to explore their values, and to me the definition that rings true is that values are *the things that are important to you*. They may be things you are currently living or things you wish you had more of in your life.

There is no judgement in values — they are not bad or good — they're just what is important to you. Others will have different values from you and that isn't bad or good, it just is. Recognising these differences allows us to understand why we get really excited about certain things while we may be nonchalant about others. On the flipside, your friends and colleagues will also hold certain things in high regard that you couldn't really care less about.

Exploring what our values are is a great exercise for two reasons:

1. *Clarity of language:* describing what matters to us, here and now in the current context of our lives, makes it easier to share this with others.

2. *Clarity of what we can let go of:* part of this exercise involves delving deeper to get clear on what our values are and what we're engaging with that actually matters to others — either other people or society as a whole. But if our actions aren't aligned with our values, they'll end up draining us. Name them and let 'em go.

Defining your values is about understanding your current context and putting a voice and a language to the things that are important in your world. The first step is to dive deep into what's uniquely important to you.

DEFINING YOUR VALUES IS ABOUT UNDERSTANDING YOUR CURRENT CONTEXT AND PUTTING A VOICE AND A LANGUAGE TO THE THINGS THAT ARE IMPORTANT IN YOUR WORLD.

EXPLORE YOUR UNIQUE BLEND

When asked to outline what matters, we can slip into default settings and respond with broad terms like 'health', 'family' and 'friends'.

These might be true values for you, but I want to call them 'boring' and irrelevant — not because they don't matter but because they don't provide any uniqueness that describes how these areas of your life matter to you. What is it about 'family' that is specifically important to you? Is it a sense of belonging? Is it an ambition that you all share? Is it the way Auntie Mary gets everyone up dancing before the night is out? These same questions go for 'health', 'friends' and any of the other broad statements you find yourself saying. To get clear on what your values are, you need to delve much deeper. You need to get interested in your unique blend.

Defining your values is similar to the art of wine appreciation, which falls on a continuum from just simply appreciating the fact that you have wine — and the more in the glass the better — up to the subtle, exquisite palette and passion that a wine aficionado brings to the table.

When you start exploring the world of wine, you can feel pretty ignorant, really only recognising that there's red and white (and the good stuff with bubbles for special occasions). As your knowledge expands beyond the bargain bin, you can start to tell a sweet from a dry white, and how the full body of a merlot is clearly different from a lighter shiraz. The deeper you go into wine appreciation, the more your palette notices the distinct flavours and nuances in each class of wine.

The same is true for starting your values exploration. Dig deeper than those broader terms and identify why these aspects are important in your life. In terms of your work, what parts light you up the most? Do you love the connections you make? Are you passionate about creating ideas? Do you love nothing more than seeing a spreadsheet mapped out? Pay attention to where your focus drifted today and write down what you uncover. Over the coming days, notice the moments that energise you. Catch yourself in these moments and pay attention to why they matter.

IDENTIFY YOUR VALUES

From the following values list,[3] circle the words that connect with you as being important in your life right now. These values may relate to things happening now or they may be things that you wish you had more of.

Highlight any of the following that are relevant for you.

Achievement	Fame	Power and authority
Adventure	Financial security	Recognition
Arts	Freedom	Self-respect
Challenge	Friendship	Spirituality
Community	Family and belonging	Status
Competence	Independence	Trust
Competition	Influencing others	Wealth
Creativity	Leadership	Wisdom
Efficiency	Openness and honesty	Work quality
Expertise	Personal development	Work under pressure

Other: _____

3 As well as this list, a bunch of great values-finding tools and assessments are available. Personally, I'm trained to deliver the AVI (A Values Inventory) and find this a robust, valid and reliable tool. My suggestion would be to grab an expert and take the time to dig deep. The effort you put in here will give you the pathway to combat Burn Out and move forward.

From your list of highlighted words, choose the top five values that are relevant for you right now:

1 _____ _____

2 _____

3 _____

4 _____ _____

5 _____

When you say these five values out loud, they need to resonate deeply with you. Picture what they mean to you. As you reflect on these words, consider how these values come to life for you. If you value family, how does this value drive your decision-making? What is it about family that's important to you? Are your values aligned to your current actions?

Listen to the rumblings

We're often told that what we starve decreases and what we feed increases. In fact, a Native American story talks about the two wolves that live inside us—a good wolf and a bad wolf—and how the one that gets bigger is the one you feed. But sometimes what you starve actually gets louder. If you've ever decided to remove sugar from your diet, you'll know how loudly your body reacts (oh, and make sure you don't need to think or function in society for a few days if you embark on this crusade). Being starved of something you crave just makes the craving stronger, louder and all-consuming. And unlike sugar cravings, cravings for your values don't go away.

WHEN WE STARVE THE KEY VALUES IN OUR LIVES, THEY DEMAND ATTENTION.

When we starve the key values in our lives, they demand attention, but they can disguise themselves in mini-tantrums. As I was writing this book, I had plenty of mini-tantrums as I battled with the sheer weight of a lengthy to-do list. I remember sitting at a cafe in tears, frustratingly believing I'd never finish this book — because when was I ever going to find the time? Without the guidance of a great friend, I would have blamed everyone else for my reaction. Instead, this beautiful friend asked me what I felt like I was ignoring.

The answer was that I was ignoring time with my kids, I was ignoring the message that I knew needed to be written in these pages, and I was ignoring the waxing appointment I'd put off three times. It was time to make time for these things — to listen to the rumblings and schedule them into my calendar.

KNOW WHAT PRESSES YOUR BUTTONS

One of the other ways we get clearer on our values — the things that are important to us — is to pay attention to the things that press our buttons. These are the things that annoy you, frustrate you and leave you feeling down right pissed off. Write down the things that press your buttons and, over the next week, notice if any of these moments come up. For me, what presses my buttons is when others talk over the top of others, fake-listen (do all the non-verbals, like nodding, but are really only thinking about which sushi they'll choose off the train tonight), or hear but don't actually comprehend what's been said. Listening is not simply waiting for your turn to talk! Arghh. This kind of behaviour gets me. Every. Single. Time.

What presses your buttons? Something does — that thing that frustrates you beyond just being vaguely annoyed, and moves into tear-your-hair-out, are-you-seriously-kidding frustration. The things that press your buttons (okay, we all know there might be more than one thing) provide clues to what matters to you — they are often frustrating because they contravene a key value. For me, the behaviours I described frustrate me because they directly hit up against my value of 'sharing and listening'. Being able to talk to my team about how the importance of everyone having air time at our meetings stems from the fact that I value sharing and listening to different perspectives is useful. When you can articulate the value that gets rattled when your buttons get pressed, you have the language you need to explain to others why this is important.

EXPLORE YOUR TOP FIVE LISTS

Have you ever played the top five game? It's a game our family regularly plays when we're sitting around the camp fire, and the rules are pretty simple: all you need is you, company, a comfy camp chair and enough wood to keep the campfire burning. Someone suggests a topic — anything from movies of all time, to places to visit, to meals you've ever had — and everyone else has to come up with their top five. (So 'top five movies of all time', and so on.)

As you get more concrete around your values, you can explore your responses to these top five lists, looking at how your responses are connected to the things that matter to you. For example:

» What are your top five movies?

» What are your top five books?

» What are your top five quotes or sayings?

How do your choices reflect your values?

Remember: when it comes to your five key values, knowing these off by heart with certainty and conviction allows you to get closer to understanding your unique blend of what's important.

Reconnect with those things that are truly important to you right here and now. Consider what action you can take today that will be connected to your values and then schedule those things in. Knowing what is important to you is the most important thing.

The bullshit of balance

In a time when obesity is at an all-time high (a recent study found that the obese now outnumber the malnourished 2:1 across the planet), we are more medicated than we've ever been and rates of chronic disease are on the rise, the cost of being in Burn Out is evident. The way to combat Burn Out is to come back to what matters to us — to define our values so they shift from being obscure to becoming clear in our lives.

Just finding 'balance' is not the answer because that implies that we need to divide up our time equally across the week. Instead, imbalance your life towards what you love — tip the scales in favour of your values. Reconnect with the things that are important to you here and now. Think about what actions you can take today that will connect you more with your values, and then do it. With greater clarity about what matters to you, the next step is to design your life so that these values are amplified. This is covered in the next chapter.

Life hack: Stop before you start

Here's a life hack to help you work out what you could stop, so that you have the space to take on something else.

The idea

When we take on new work projects, we take on more stuff, and doing so can sometimes feel like trying to squeeze more air out of an accordion that is already deflated. Rather than take on more, you first need to stop something else to create space for the new tasks.

The action

Consider the following things you could stop and ask yourself: what would I gain and what would I lose?

Actions to stop	What do you gain?	What do you lose?
Stop watching TV after 8 pm		
Stop internet/wi-fi at home for 2 hours/days		
Stop staying up after 9:30 pm		
Stop taking your phone out with you		
Stop doing all the cleaning at home		
Stop eating take away food		
Stop going to every meeting		
Stop taking work home		
Stop sending emails after hours		
Stop answering the phone every time it rings		

What could you commit to stopping to create more space and time?

CHAPTER 7
Design a values-aligned life

Oprah famously has a quote on the wall outside her office that reads, 'You are responsible for the energy you bring into this room.' In 2015, I was fortunate enough to see Oprah perform a solo event to a sell-out crowd in Brisbane, Australia. One of the many lessons she shared from her rich journey was the power of living with intentions — and this can be from the intention we set for the day ahead when we lift our head off the pillow to the intention we set at the start of our team meetings. She confirmed her stance that we are all personally responsible for the energy we bring into any room that we enter. When that energy is plugged into the clarity of knowing what's important to you here and now, it's a powerful force.

When we're sitting in Burn Out, we can be so caught up in the busyness of action that to stop, pause and set an intention sits at the very bottom of our to-do list (waaayyyy below even clearing out the limp lettuce in the fridge). That is, unless we have been purposeful about designing a life that amplifies those things that are important to us.

The second action in combatting Burn Out is to take the values that we have defined as being important, and bring these values to life. If we don't — if all we do is simply articulate what matters but do nothing with them — we diminish the power and impact they can have. They become words on a page or a plaque on the wall that gathers dust but holds zero meaning beyond that. Stepping fully into your values requires stadium-filling amplification.

From diminished to amplified

Coldplay are arguably one of the greatest bands of our time, maybe ever. If you ever get a chance to attend a Coldplay concert, run don't walk. It is an epic experience. The atmosphere they create through their music and the choreography of lights, their sheer talent and their energy is electric. They not only own the stage, but for the hours they are present they also own the whole stadium and surrounding suburbs. That's the power of switched-on, turned-up amplification.

It would serve no-one for Chris Martin and the Coldplay crew to dial back their talent, to whisper their songs and downplay their passion. We'd all miss out. And yet, in our day-to-day life we do this with the things that are important to us. In a world of politeness and inclusion, even when our values are clear, we don't want to be seen as imposing our values onto others. We don't want the backlash of others not buying into what we're pitching. And the result is we keep our values hidden.

As noble as this sentiment is, it means we end up diminishing our values rather than standing their sacred ground. To combat that — to turn the volume switch to full bore and move from diminishing to amplifying the 'why' — the key is to design values-aligned actions.

Designing a values-aligned life happens across four areas:

1. your intentions
2. your behaviours
3. your environment
4. your rituals.

YOUR INTENTION DRIVES YOUR ATTENTION

As Oprah shared, intention setting has become part of her daily routine. The reason is that setting our intention drives our attention. The impact of shifting from busy task to busy task without getting clear on our intention is that our attention is left completely up for grabs. If we don't control where our attention goes, it is open to being dragged into any urgent thing that appears in front of us. If you've ever found yourself down a Google search rabbit warren — you know, where you started looking at local restaurants for Friday night, and soon you're filling out a questionnaire to find out which actor would play you in a movie (and you've somehow made three online purchases along the way) — then you've experienced an attention hijacking. While this can be okay occasionally, research is now finding that we are collectively struggling to stick to task because of the dopamine release we experience ticking off a million little things, ignoring the important thing that we want to get done.

SETTING OUR INTENTION DRIVES OUR ATTENTION.

Sit in the driver's seat of your focus by setting a clear intention. If your intention is to support the new staff member in the team, your attention is on taking the time to connect with them at the start of the day, and to be aware if they look confused or lost. Pausing to set your intention, whether that means a quick ten seconds before a phone call or five minutes at the start of a meeting, will change what not only you, but also the people around you focus on too.

Our values give meaning to the mundane tasks of our lives. While working in the Northern Territory, Australia, I was mentoring a senior executive for a government organisation. Before we started our sessions, his manager spoke to me about how my client was terrible at finishing his paperwork, so much so that not only would he avoid all administrative tasks but he would also actually delete any emails asking him to do them. He wanted me to incorporate dealing with this into my sessions somehow.

Not one to beat someone around the head for not doing their paperwork, I dismissed this request and got to work on the more interesting conversations. My client completed a values assessment, and one of his top values was being able to 'support people do their job better'. This was a key part of his role working in communities across the Northern Territory, and absolutely one of the areas he felt fulfilled in doing.

On our third session, he came in and said, 'Al, this values stuff is really interesting. I've had a realisation: when I get an email from interstate asking for me to complete paperwork, there's someone who can't do their job until I've completed it. So I've been doing my paperwork every time I'm asked'. For him, being able to connect this mundane task of doing boring paperwork to one of his top values of supporting people to do their job gave him a greater sense of meaning.

When we're sitting in Burn Out, the goal is not necessarily about making less progress; it's about finding more meaning in the tasks we're already doing — reigniting the drive and connecting our actions with our purpose.

YOUR BEHAVIOURS SHOW YOUR INTENTIONS

Pausing and setting your intention is important, but doing so is useless if your behaviour doesn't follow. What we do, our behaviours, speak louder than what we say. As a parent, my words sometimes don't match my own behaviours — like yelling, 'Stop shouting!' at my fighting kids. (Yep, that'll teach 'em.)

In our workplaces, we see this kind of mismatch all the time. At the extreme, it's the organisation that espouses health and vitality while its people work overtime in poor conditions. It's the boss who states they have an 'open-door' policy, but bites the head off any team member who interrupts them during the day. Values are brought to life by the behaviours we engage in.

In your life, if one of your values is connection to family, getting clear on what that looks like, and what you need to be doing to bring that to life, is key. In order to amplify values rather than diminish them, and in order to design a values-aligned life, we need to get clear on the behaviours that matter. The behaviours that we are going to hold ourselves accountable to. And then go do 'em.

Traits versus behaviours

Before diving into an exploration of values-aligned behaviours, it's important to get clear on the definition of behaviours and the confusion relating to this that can happen in our language. This is a concept that makes sense on the surface but, when we dig a bit deeper, rarely can we clearly articulate specific behaviours that we are going to engage in.

I'm the director of Pragmatic Thinking,[1] a behaviour and motivation strategy company, and one of the key areas that our company is built on is supporting leaders and individuals in organisations to have the tough conversations. Confusion is often rife in conversations that are sensitive, personal and, well, just plain tough. One of the reasons for this confusion is the use of trait-based language rather than behaviour-based language.

---

1 Seriously, the work we do with organisations around the world is way cool. Check it out for yourself at www.pragmaticthinking.com.

In our best-selling book *Dealing with the Tough Stuff*, we unpack the difference between traits and behaviours, and it's useful to revisit this distinction here:

Do you know people who you describe as adventurous or lazy or unreliable? These descriptors are traits. A trait is merely a label — usually a descriptor of a combination of behaviours. For example, if someone is considered courteous, that would be a trait. It is a convenient way to describe a collection of behaviours, such as holding a door open for someone, wishing people good morning, or asking people if they would like anything at the shops. A behaviour is something that is directly observable. A trait is usually a combination of behaviours.

The more specific you can be about the behaviours that will bring your values to life, the easier it is to commit to and engage in these behaviours, and the easier it is to hold yourself (or have someone else hold you) accountable for these too. For example, rather than simply connecting with the value of 'generosity' (you can display this in infinite ways), get clear on where, when and with whom you want to be generous. This could be baking cupcakes for the team every Thursday, spending time at a local soup kitchen once a month, or 'liking' every picture in your Instagram feed (go, you good Samaritan)! This part is fun, because this is where you get to play with the actions of what matters. Do it your way, do it differently, smear your personality over what you're going to commit to.

Exploring behaviours is easier when you are clear on the context. For example, are you being generous at work, at home or with the weekend sporting team? Would you prefer to be generous with your time, generous in sharing the information you know, or generous in connecting people with the contacts you have? Know the value (generosity), clarify the context (social media) and define the behaviour (liking *everything*).

Here I outline a simple process to get clear on the specific behaviours you want to engage in, and you can also use this process with a team within your workplace too. Write down your value, get clear on the context, and then jot down potential behaviours. For example, the value might be caring and the context might be customers. A potential behaviour might be to send a thank you card and the new book by their favourite author.

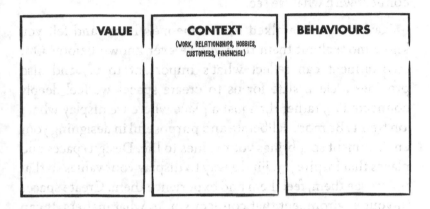

VALUE	CONTEXT (WORK, RELATIONSHIPS, HOBBIES, CUSTOMERS, FINANCIAL)	BEHAVIOURS

To clarify the behaviours you are going to step into in order to design a values-aligned life, ask yourself the following questions:

- » What does that behaviour look like?
- » What would I or others see if I was living out this value?
- » What are possible behaviours that would reflect this value in different contexts?

YOUR ENVIRONMENT REFLECTS YOUR VALUES

Corporate anthropologist Michael Henderson from Cultures at Work has spent his career studying cultures around the world and relating his findings to the corporate setting.[2] One

---

2   Michael's work is cutting edge, and he also has the most amazing sit-round-a-camp-fire-and-share-stories kinda voice that you just want to listen to all day. Google his video clips and you'll see what I mean.

of the things all cultures have in common (including some of the world's oldest cultures like Indigenous Australian tribes and Zulu warriors) is the signs and symbols that identify what's important to them — from artwork to stories, and tools to totems. When it comes to amplifying values, go visual. We connect with what we see.

Have you ever walked into someone's home and felt you know more about them than you've ever known before? Our environment can reflect what's important to us, and also provides a clean slate for us to create spaces we feel deeply connected to, rather than just a place where we display what's 'on trend'. Be more deliberate and purposeful in designing your environment so it brings your values to life. Design spaces and places that inspire joy. Find a way to display your values so that others see them, feel them and experience them. Create spaces in your environment that connect you to what matters. It can be anything from photos of moments that mattered, to pictures that capture meaning for you and artefacts that hold meaning.

Get your art on

This is your time to get creative, and there is no judgement here. What you create doesn't have to be perfect; it just has to connect with you. Design it your way, and play with the art of expressing your heart. The following list (overleaf) provides some ideas on how you can bring your values to life in physical forms. Ask yourself the question, what does that look like?

PLAY WITH THE ART OF EXPRESSING YOUR HEART.

Get your art on and find meaning in the spaces around you through the following:

» Write down the movies or TV series that resonate with your values. Carve out time to reconnect with these movies and series.

» Create a playlist of songs that depict your values.

» Take and/or find pictures that you love and put them up.

» Find ways to dress according to what matters to you.

» Accessorise for activities — if writing matters to you, for example, get yourself a beautiful notebook.

» Create zones that reconnect you to your values (whether this is in the home, garden, park, car, work or the man-shed).

» Share the symbols of your values with others (through social media, emails or gifts).

Work environments

In the work environment, we want others to buy into the team or organisational values, so the power of bringing values to life there is key. Connect with experts and designers, and collaborate with creatives who can help you bring these ideas and behaviours to life visually. Make sure, though, that the end result reflects the people who work there and the values the organisation stands for. Don't put in a slide and a table tennis table simply because Google HQ has one, for example. Create something that rings true for you. Create your own trademark in the work space.

In the work that we do at Pragmatic Thinking, we know that behaviour and motivation at work are closely influenced by design. Having a killer set of values can live and die by how they are shared. Typing them into an email or simply putting them onto a letterhead doesn't make them inspiring. Instead, partnering with designers can be the outlet for you to bring values to life through beautiful visual elements within posters, coasters, question cards, notebooks, stickers and even comics. In this way, organisational values become tangible and tactile — inspiring your people to not only be proud of them, but also live and breathe them at work and with clients.

RITUALS ARE YOUR ANCHOR

Rituals and routines give us an anchor in the busyness. We tend to get so busy that the important things get shoved to the bottom of the pile, added to the never-ending to-do list. So when things are crazy in this state of Burn Out — when that overwhelm hits us — those routines and rituals give us something to hold onto. They are the anchor in the storm. When I talk to people and clients, I often hear that they constantly feel like they're being pulled in a million different directions, and this is certainly also true in my own experience. It may be that those different directions are actually all really interesting and we want to sink our teeth into all of them, but the result is we end up just flip-flopping between a whole range of different things, making millimetres of progress in a few different directions, but really getting nowhere with anything in particular.

Once you've gotten clear on the behaviours you are going to engage in, and you've created tangible reminders of those things that matter in your space, rituals are the things that pulse and keep your values alive.

Use these three actions to turn your ideas into rituals:

1. *Schedule it:* we grossly overestimate how much time we have and underestimate how long things will take us. Which is why, when we put the stuff that matters to the end it never gets done. Flip that notion and put the things that matter into your calendar. Take five minutes on Sunday evening to schedule in the actions that matter for you this week. If it's a morning ritual, set yourself a time you can commit to; if it's a yoga class, block the time out; if it's an adventure with friends square it away. Once these activities that matter are in the schedule, they become your default, and you no longer have to make a decision. Honour the schedule and notice how your week changes.

2. *Share it:* find someone who can hold you accountable to this ritual. This is a person you trust who will check in on how it went, without judgement, but with the caring accountability to keep pulling you back to yourself.

3. *Tweak it:* adapt your ritual to still fit in when life changes. For example, what changes with your ritual when you're on holidays? How can you keep it up when you have to travel for work? Tweak it so it doesn't get dropped into the too-hard basket and become a good idea you had once but that never came to anything.

You've got to fight and nudge for these moments in your week. Imagine you're in a mosh pit with a million people, trying to get to the front of the stage. How do you just graciously and slowly but very persistently elbow your way through the busyness? How do you still stake out your ground and make a claim in that space? By designing your intention, setting your behaviours, crafting your environment and committing to your rituals, you can gently nudge and elbow your way back to those things that matter to you.

Refresh and redesign

Your 'why' can and will change, so having the foresight to invest in a redesign to refresh the palette is important. Google any brand more than 50 years old and you'll see the changes and iterations the branding has undergone — from visual changes to their logo to the change in focus of their work. The same is true for the internal work.

When you find yourself back in the grind, where the initial love of what you do every day has worn off, look for ways to refresh and redesign your intention, shake up the behaviours, revamp the environment and reset new rituals. Do this and it will keep what really matters alive.

Life hack: Temptation bundling

Here's a life hack to help you stop delaying what you love while still getting done what you have to.

The idea

Temptation bundling is an approach coined by Katherine Milkman from The Wharton School at the University of Pennsylvania that ties together two activities — an activity that you 'should' be doing but may be avoiding and an activity that you want to do. For example, you could bundle having a pedicure with catching up on emails on your laptop, or you could finish off a report with a coffee at your favourite cafe, or clean the kitchen while listening to your favourite band.

The action

Temptation bundling starts with taking an audit on those tasks that either you are currently putting off, or that you resent having to do. Ask yourself *what am I stuck on?*, and without editing write down a list of these things.

Once you've got your list go back over it with fresh eyes and consider what enjoyable activity you could bundle, pair, it up with. Get creative in your thinking about how you can pair these activities that you 'need' to do, with something you 'want' to do. Rather than have the reward afterwards, find a way to make the task inherently rewarding.

Brainstorm your new project with a friend, smash out emails with your favourite smoothie, wash the car with your favourite tunes blaring out loud. Make the mundane just a little more tempting.

CHAPTER 8
Defend the sacred

Conferences and seminars are a big part of my world. Sitting in them, speaking at them, organising them (not to mention judging the quality of their morning teas; seriously — don't be scrimping on those scones, people). The insights and the learnings from these events can shift your thinking and have a significant impact on what you do when you get back to so-called life as usual. The importance of defending what's sacred and making time for what matters was a lesson that hit me as I was sitting in the audience of a seminar a number of years ago.

The speaker was a highly sought-after social sciences researcher. The truth is I can't recall his name, or even the research he was sharing; what I do recall was his personal commitment to his health, even in a busy position. He shared with us that his personal non-negotiable was to do 30 minutes of exercise every single day. While this might not sound like much, with global travel and hours of back-to-back meetings, this non-negotiable was challenged daily. He shared how he cut short a significant meeting with the CEO, CFO and executives of a big organisation because he had to do his half hour of exercise. They tried to dismiss this but he didn't back down. His commitment to protect the sacred ground of what mattered to him, his health, so that his contribution could continue to be world-class struck me. When you get clear on what matters, you've got to work hard to protect it.

At times your values will be tested, and you'll be asked to guard these values against forces that try to sway them or knock them into irrelevancy. When this happens, you'll need to go into battle on behalf of those whispers that nudge you — to honour them and find protection for them. Because unless you defend what is sacred to you, you will be exposed to the elements of busy, lashed at by other people's priorities. It'll leave you dizzier then a two-year-old in a tea-cup ride at the local country show, not sure which way is up. Remember: your values are your true north.

The hard work around values isn't in finding out what they are; the hard work is defending them in a world with competing priorities. In my work, I've seen well-intentioned teams and leaders dedicate time, resources and effort to exploring what really matters to them, and aligning this with organisational strategy — only to then let this work gather dust in the corner as they go about their 'real work'. The individuals, teams and organisations who bring their values to life in a way that they become enmeshed in their identity and reputation are the ones who also commit to this step in the process — that is, they defend them incessantly.

We are drawn to people, teams and brands who know with certainty who they are, and are proud to shout it from the rooftops. Stop apologising for being passionate about what matters; be vulnerable enough to get over feeling embarrassed by who you are, even if it's dramatically different from others. All too often I see people playing it cool, and hiding and downplaying their values for fear that others may ridicule the very thing that sits at the core of who they are. If you don't honour, uphold and love these truths about you, others won't either. It starts with you defending what's sacred in your life.

From exposed to protected

Busy can be armour we wear to protect us from facing the thing that really matters, providing a legitimate reason to put off or avoid the conversations we need to have with others. In a busy world, getting caught up in our ever-growing to-do list is not only seen as okay, but it's also rewarded. Here's the thing, though — defaulting to going through email distracts us from doing the hard work of standing for what matters. Checking our phones the moment we step out of a meeting stops us from connecting with the person walking out next to us. Rushing to our next meeting gets in the way of us having that boundary-setting conversation we know we need to have.

To defend your values, to hold true to the anchor of what matters to you — truly matters to you — you need to hold back the tide of busy and be purposeful about where your energy and your focus go. Doing so can actually move you from feeling exposed to feeling protected — so you don't need the flimsy armour of busy anyway. Because the thing is this armour of busy is a false shield. It's as useful at protecting us as putting on moisturiser in the sunshine. No matter how much you put on you'll still get burnt.

And when your focus gets sucked back into the vortex of email dings, comments on your latest social media post, or obsessing about whether you should get the blue or the purple wrapping paper, pause and ask, 'Is this the best use of my time right now?' Centre yourself by protecting what matters, and dropping the rest.

LET GO OF #FOMO

Part of what keeps us on the treadmill of busy is we get asked to do a million things and say (usually in our high-pitched, saying-yes-because-I-should voice), 'Sure thing' right before the tsunami of regret kicks in. When it comes to defending our most important currency, our time, we drop our guard.

Saying no is hard. It's hard because, as the modern-day peeps say, we can slide into #FOMO (fear of missing out). If everyone else is having a great time (or at least looking like they're having a great time, based on the photos they post on Instagram #YOLO (you only live once)) and I'm not part of it, I must be on the outer. Even if doing something doesn't feel right or is going to drain us, we usually end up saying yes anyway and stretching ourselves too thin. Why? Because we fear that saying no will end the asking.

For me, the fear of saying 'No, not now', and so knocking back an opportunity, ignites the internal gremlins that ask, 'But what if you never get asked again?' 'What if the work enquiries stop coming through the door?', 'What if my friends move on?' With a jam-packed calendar and multiple trips away from home, blocking out time on a quieter week to hang with my kids and recharge feels selfish and indulgent, yet it is absolutely aligned to my values. Letting go of #FOMO and owning our values-based choices is critical to combatting Burn Out.

When you set these clear lines in the sand, others have permission to do the same. You become known as the person who won't stretch themselves too thin, who is really present when they turn up because regret doesn't follow them around. Your 'yes' carries far more weight because you can deliver on your commitment. Ironically, that's the kind of person a manager looks for on their team and it's the kind of person your friends admire. Drop the #FOMO and you'll find that it's because of this stance that the opportunities keep coming back.

Draw the line

It's time to draw the line and go boss-like on our lives. The quickest way we can defend our values is to ensure our behaviours — the actions that we engage in on a regular basis — are aligned with what matters to us. In order to do this, we need to get forensic about where we're actually spending our time. Get curious about where your attention is drawn towards and what it's drawn away from. This will give you a clue about the current behaviours you want to defend and the behaviours that can be shifted.

> **THE QUICKEST WAY WE CAN DEFEND OUR VALUES IS TO ENSURE OUR BEHAVIOURS — THE ACTIONS THAT WE ENGAGE IN ON A REGULAR BASIS — ARE ALIGNED WITH WHAT MATTERS TO US.**

Take a moment to grab a piece of paper and write down the activities in your week that drain you. What are the things you feel like you're dragging your heels on? Or what's the stuff that you keep putting off? Write down anything that comes to mind. It doesn't matter if it's having to wash the dishes verses having to call clients about a project. Whatever it is, as big or as small it is, I want you to write it down. The longer the list, the better.

When we understand our current default way of behaving, we can be strategic about whether these behaviours are serving us or not. Review your list through the lens of three actions that will free up time and energy: sort out what you can mitigate (reduce the impact of), delegate (hand over responsibility for) or eliminate (remove all together).

MITIGATE THE IMPACT

Mitigating tasks means reducing the gravity or the impact of them. The reduction might be in the impact on your thinking or productivity, or on how you feel. Mitigation is the first step in reducing the impact of the tasks that drain you. Your focus isn't on stopping doing them but on changing how you do them. For example, rather than have continual interruptions at work, set clear times when you're available and clear times that are peak productivity for you and explain that you're not available during those time. Or instead of having coffee catch-ups that may go longer than you anticipated, catch up with a friend over a walk-and-talk. Or instead of putting off mundane administration tasks, engineer a game for yourself — do them for 20 minutes and then you can have a tea break. Look at your procrastination list and identify the tasks you have to do but could redesign how you do them so they are more engaging. From a mindset perspective, if you mitigate tasks in three main areas, you will see a significant impact on how you face your day.

The first starts with addressing the internal guilt of 'should'. Whenever we use the word should — 'Oh, I should lose those 5 kilos', 'I should work back late', 'I should spend more time with my kids' — guilt always tags along for the ride, like an unwelcome passenger, leaving us feeling bad. Guilt doesn't serve us to get into action. And piling ourselves full of 'shoulds' certainly doesn't serve us to Stand Out. Mitigate the hold that 'should' has on your internal thinking.

Second, mitigation requires sitting down with our inner critic and telling it who's boss. Self-flagellation has no place in building a Stand Out life. Now, working hard is different from beating yourself up. They're two separate things, but often we work hard and in the process still say, 'Oh, I didn't quite get around to that. I could have done that better. It's not quite good enough'. With all that constant internal chatter, we fall into bed at night feeling bad about ourselves — because that's what we've heard all day. We need to mitigate the impact this internal critic has on us and instead celebrate turning up and putting in the effort we did.

The third thing we need to mitigate is the time we spend with dream stealers. You know who they are: the people who when you talk about your dreams or where you want to go, seem to feel like it's their job to poke as many holes in that dream as they possibly can. They leave you feeling drained, don't they? Maybe you can't actually get some of these people out of your life — they're family, work colleagues or the barista who serves your morning coffee with a side order of contempt (but you keep going back because no-one brews coffee like they do). We can't rid them from our lives, but we can mitigate the impact they have. Sometimes that's about protecting your dreams by not pouring your whole heart out to those people, but instead finding common ground to talk about what's important to them. You can talk about the weather. You can talk about who's winning the footy. Whatever it is, find ways to mitigate around that.

DELEGATE LIKE A BOSS

Defending your values means you have to master the art of delegation — that is, entrusting tasks and responsibilities to someone else. Delegating is hard because others will do the tasks differently from you — they may take longer, they may go down a different path, and they may make mistakes. Handing stuff over can be one of the scariest tasks you take on, but it's a crucial skill. The people you hold in high regard — whatever their field of expertise — have all mastered it. Not only do they know how to delegate well, but they also have clarity about what to delegate and what tasks fall squarely in their lap.

It can be challenging, but don't dismiss the importance of delegation. Mastering the art will give you the space and time to step into the actions that matter and the areas where you can make the biggest difference.

Over many years Gallup researched thousands of great leaders from across the world, and from various industries, with the goal of articulating the top three to five qualities all great leaders share.[1] Because, of course, when we know what these qualities are, we can teach them to emerging leaders and they will, by default, become great leaders. This sounds great in theory.

What Gallup actually found was fascinating. They found that no consistent set of qualities is common to great leaders. Leadership styles, personalities, characters and qualities were as varied as the leaders studied. But the one thing the great leaders had in common was their certainty around their strengths, and they engineered their work to ensure they operated within these strengths most of the time. They then outsourced the rest. If their job required them to be financially savvy, and this wasn't a key strength for them, they'd build a team around them that filled that gap.

We can learn from these leaders who have clarity about their greatest contribution and find ways to delegate the rest. I believe you need to delegate any task where 80 per cent or up to 80 per cent is fine. If output needs to be 100 per cent, and you've got 100 per cent responsibility and risk, this task likely falls in your lap. But if all you need to do is either oversee the task or you don't really need to be involved at all, find a way to delegate it.

We live in an era where you can outsource pretty much anything, to anyone, even for a short period of time. This trend is growing. If you just need someone to do some transcribing for you, you can get that done while you sleep and it's ready when you wake in the morning. If you need someone to organise an Excel spreadsheet for you, you can get it done with a few clicks of your mouse.

We also need to delegate anything that enables others. Remember: there are no martyrs here. If that means getting your

---

1   You can read about the results in **Strengths Based Leadership**, published in 2009.

kids to clean their room rather than you begrudgingly doing so, do that. Give them the opportunity to be enabled to clean up, or to help with preparing and cooking meals once they're old enough. (You want them to move out at some point, don't you?) Delegate anything that will help others to grow. No-one can learn a skill or how to do new things if you keep doing it for them.

So delegate the tasks that you can still oversee and have influence on but where the ultimate outcome doesn't have to fall to you.

ELIMINATE IT, STAT

You can cut some tasks and actions out altogether. Here are three categories to get you started on what you can eliminate:

1. *Eliminate the goals you serially ignore:* if you keep writing down certain goals but don't get around to doing them, put these goals to the values test. Are they really important to you, but you're not getting any traction on them? Then we'll unpack how to make progress in the Freak Out section. If, on the other hand, they are fun but not really connected to the core of who you are, it's time to let them go. This is not a bad thing — clearly at this stage, the task isn't a high priority, so stop feeling guilty about it.

2. *Eliminate any activities that are no longer serving you:* don't keep doing something just because it's the way it's always been done. Instead, get rid of it. Is there anything on your 'what drains you' list you might be able to eliminate? For example, ironing tea towels could definitely be on this list — they don't need it, no-one notices it, and wrinkled tea towels dry just as well.

3. *Eliminate people who drain you:* I'm talking metaphorically here, not literally, of course. Focus on spending time with people who are going to lift you up, who inspire you,

and are going to be your champions to moving toward. It's not about dismissing people from your world, but consciously gravitating towards those who leave you feeling better about yourself.

Return to your 'what drains you' list and put M for mitigate, D for delegate or E for eliminate against each item. Imagine the time and space you'd have to focus on the stuff that energises you if you were to mitigate, delegate or eliminate these things — because 'busy' doesn't have to be a part of your story.

The badge of busy is not serving us or anyone. I want you to put your hand on your heart, raise your other hand in the air and repeat after me: 'I promise,' (I'm waiting for you to say it). 'I promise to never again — *never again* — say that I'm busy when someone asks me how I am.'

Brilliant. Now I want you to come up with another way of answering that question — an answer that is actually going to leave you feeling uplifted. That's your one simple task from this lesson: stop making 'busy' your default and come up with an uplifting statement for when people ask you how you are. Be inventive. Say, 'You know what? I'm cranking things out and hitting some really cool targets' or 'I'm creating something that's never been created before, and I'm really excited about it'. Notice how different that feels to say? Defend the sacred energy of your words.

PUT A VOICE TO YOUR VALUES, DESIGN THEM TO BE EMBEDDED IN YOUR LIFE AND THEN PROTECT THEM FROM BOTH OUTSIDE INFLUENCES AND DIRECT ATTACKS.

When you've mitigated, delegated or eliminated those things on your 'what drains me' list, it's time to declare what matters. Put a voice to your values, design them to be embedded in your life and then protect them from both outside influences and direct attacks.

Leadership: defend what's sacred in your workplace

If you're a leader in your workplace or you run your own business, your ability to treat your values as sacred is critical for the people you lead. Simon Sinek is a world-renowned speaker and author of the best-selling books *Start with Why* and *Leaders Eat Last*. In his current research, he talks about the responsibility of leaders to create safe environments, particularly in environments of high change, shifting customer base and rapid technology advances.

Values provide the anchor that individuals, teams and leaders can hold onto among the noise and uncertainty. As a leader, you need to know your own and the team's values off by heart and defend their sacredness. In chapter 9 we'll step through how.

SET NON-NEGOTIABLES

In a team and group setting, jointly clarify expected behaviours, and agree to hold each other to account. The key is to create a set of non-negotiable behaviours that align with values. And remember: when exploring non-negotiables you should include no more than five behaviours, because if everything becomes important, nothing is important.

In our business, every position has a set of non-negotiable behaviours that are relevant to that role as well as '10 ways to make us love you' — that is, nice-to-have behaviours. But these nice-to-haves never replace the non-negotiable behaviours. Providing clarity of expected behaviours ensures people are aligned with a values-focused way of working.

MAKE IT PUBLIC

Declare it out loud. This sounds obvious, but so many leaders and organisations simply post their values on a plaque or on a page on their website, and then everywhere else they remain hidden. Embed your values into every touchpoint with clients and every discussion within the team, and get visual with them in your waiting room, interview room and business cards.

CELEBRATE AND REWARD

Catch people out when they act in alignment with your organisation's values, and celebrate and reward the efforts of coming together. If your team's values are connected to 'creative ideation', as the leader, you need to celebrate every idea that comes to the table and recognise the effort it takes to speak up, even if the idea isn't going to fly or isn't relevant. It's the idea creation itself that needs to be defended and protected.

Know the 'why' behind the 'what'

The reason we are seeking to define, design and defend our values is to move away from having 'no why' towards the space where we 'know why'. This is where we walk with a strut, shoulders back, head straight, chest out.

As my great friend Matt Church says, it's your job to be the CEO: the Chief Energy Officer. You are responsible for the energy you bring in the space. You are responsible for how you respond when crazy-busy turns up. You are responsible for pausing and reconnecting to the why of here and now. Our values get tested when we're faced with exposure and, like with our health, being exposed to toxins is not good for us. If we're not protecting our values vigilantly the toxins of busy and the priorities of others have the capacity to infect us.

Life hack: Social media elimination diet

One of the ways we can start to defend our values is to craft some time back, and this life hack looks at taking some time back from our social media habits.

The idea

What would you do if you had an extra fourteen hours every week? This could be the equivalent of a bonus weekend, every week, or two extra days of work. What could you get done that is important to you? In 2015 the English *Telegraph* newspaper published research findings that, on average, we spend 1 hour and 40 minutes every day on social media, with the majority of us having at least five different social media channels that we are a part of. And yet we struggle to find ten minutes every day to sit and notice the world around us.

The action

Start with a full social media elimination:

1. Full digital detox for a week. Delete the apps from your phone and tablets. Remove access to these channels. Even if your business or work is online, for one week you can unplug, or delegate someone else to track this for you. Notice what you feel like you're missing.

2. Gradually introduce one social media platform per week over the next three to five weeks. Make a decision about which ones are relevant for you.

3. Notice the impact that the reintroduction has to your time and attention.

Burn out wrap up

When it comes to investing in values, your goal is to make sure they shift from being obscure to clear, from diminished to amplified and from exposed to protected. To achieve this, centre your attention on these three key actions:

1. *Define what's important:* dedicate the time needed to get clear on what matters in your life now. Combat the vague, and get specific about your unique blend of values. When we can articulate what matters, and know ourselves well enough to stand behind it, we have our own battery charger to reenergise us in a busy world.

2. *Design a values-aligned life:* this is your life and you have the choice to engineer it. From your behaviours, to your environment, to the rituals of your week, find the art to express what's in your heart. No matter what comes your way, these become your anchors that bring you back to what matters in this moment.

3. *Defend the sacred:* combat the false armour of busy by defending what's sacred to you. Explore those tasks that you can mitigate, delegate or eliminate, and focus on protecting the activities that matter.

Part IV
Tackle freak out

Screw Freak Out. As Dan Sullivan says, 'All progress starts by telling the truth', so here's the truth about Freak Out. It's a shitty place to be. But, really, not that much conversation takes place about it, does it? People in the wellbeing industry, the area I have worked in, tend to spend most of their time extolling the less-than-great virtues of Check Out and (their poster child) Burn Out — and, really, for good reason. Life living in those states is not fun, and the evidence overwhelmingly shows that your health suffers markedly when you spend lengthy time in them.

But Freak Out is the silent one, like a sneaky fart after beans for brekky. You mightn't hear much about it, but it sure does have some impact. The physical effects of our ol' friend Burn Out (covered in chapter 6) are plain to see: the constantly furrowed brow, the bags under the eyes — heck even the stains on the underarm of your shirts from good old-fashioned sweat. Eeww. It's there for all and sundry to see. And Check Out? Also pretty easy to see; in most cases you're simply not there. Sometimes, you're physically not there — you're sitting on the couch or in bed instead —but in other circumstances your physical form is there, but mentally you've left the building.

But then there's Freak Out, which, quite literally, can feel like it's driving you crazy. I'm using that term not in any clinical sense, but more to capture how you can feel lost and uncertain about what to do next because nothing is happening the way you had hoped it would. We've all been in the midst of Freak Out from time to time, where we're seeing a vision of how things could be different but the abyss between here and there seems impassable.

Across the next three chapters we're going to tackle this silent state to combat its cost to our sanity, and find ways to invest in processes that will drive progress. Specifically, we're going to set out the map you need to head in the right direction, we're going to chunk your goal down so you can get into action, and we're going to make sure we see the progress that we're making.

CHAPTER 9
Map it

Here you are; your values — the essence of your heart and soul, the very things that dictate where your energy and attention go — have given you a direction in which to head. Maybe you've decided upon a new vocation of some kind (and I don't necessarily mean work; the new vocation might be a hobby or artistic pursuit, a side hustle) and you're genuinely excited to head down that path, even if it scares you a little. But there's a huge problem. You're stuck at the starting line. Nothing is happening.

So you start to question yourself at three levels. You question your desire, the value of what you are pursuing, and lastly, your self-worth. But as Elizabeth Gilbert says, 'Opportunity dances with those already on the dance floor', so let's take a look at these to start with and uncover them as the myths they truly are.

From blindfolded to blueprint

Our desire is a very common area we tend to question ourselves on, with our questioning often sounding something like this: 'Maybe you don't want it badly enough, then'.

Ouch.

I don't know about you, but that cliché riles me, and I've been caught in its web plenty of times believing that I just needed to want my goal more, and then success would come (sound the trumpets!). The truth is you can desperately want something but have no idea about how to go about obtaining it. Want proof? What about an unrequited love? I remember when I was fourteen years old. I was so infatuated with a boy — let's call him 'Brian'. I was infatuated with the way he walked, the way he talked ... the way he had no freakin' idea I even existed. It was intoxicating and he consumed the majority of my waking thoughts. Well, him and Christian Slater.

I can conclusively tell you that I wanted it badly enough.

I wanted him to look in my direction.

I wanted him to talk to me.

I wanted him to maybe even hold my hand.

To be honest I didn't really know what I wanted — I was fourteen — but I knew I wanted him to be my boyfriend. But I had no clue what to do about it. Fast forward five or six years, though, and the game was different. I had a few more ideas about what to do to start a conversation — okay, so the conversation was still clunky, with no guarantee it would work, but I knew how to kick into gear and gave it a go.

But when I was fourteen, I didn't have the skills or confidence to know where to start. Trust me: I wanted it badly enough, though. Even now, desire still doesn't guarantee success. Surfing four-foot waves, doing a headstand in yoga, cooking a three-course meal for dinner guests without a side of charcoal on every dish, for example — these desire-filled activities are all currently outside of my reality. Desire is not the *only* thing we need.

The second area where we question ourselves when we're in Freak Out is the value of our goal or vision. Why would anyone want to read what I write? Maybe no-one really wants to buy my hand-crafted jewellery? Perhaps my business venture won't get traction in the market?

Questioning the value of our offering becomes a yoke around our necks and we can continually sit in the grind of evaluation until the enthusiasm fades any great idea into obscurity. And, again, questioning the value of your pursuit is crap. Truly, it is a self-limiting belief driven by fear. I promise you that if what you produce is from your heart — the best part of you — the work wants it. It needs it. So begone doubt. You're not welcome 'ere.

The third and last area where we question ourselves is our self-worth. Someone else who's smarter, more experienced, more talented, more [insert adjective here] could do this but not *me*. Who am I?

Marianne Williamson's magnificent words acknowledge this questioning: 'Who am I to be brilliant, gorgeous, talented, and fabulous?'

Well, I'm here to answer that question. You. That's who.

Actually, the full quote from Williamson is worth reading on a daily basis, so I've included it here:

Our deepest fear is not that we are inadequate. Our deepest fear is that we are powerful beyond measure. It is our light, not our darkness that most frightens us. We ask ourselves, Who am I to be brilliant, gorgeous, talented, and fabulous? Actually, who are you not to be? You are a child of God. Your playing small does not serve the world. There is nothing enlightened about shrinking so that other people will not feel insecure around you. We are all meant to shine, as children do. We were born to make manifest the glory of God that is within us. It is not just in some of us; it is in everyone and as we let our own light shine, we unconsciously give others permission to do the same. As we are liberated from our own fear, our presence automatically liberates others.

But, whoa, we carry that fear don't we? Why me? Why should I deserve to be loved?

Don't worry—nary a word written within the pages of this book wasn't underwritten by tears, anguish and wine in equal measures. But while I heard that voice of self-doubt and protection, I refused to take orders from it.

So fight the fight in your head. Tell those voices to take a back seat. That's the first step to moving out of Freak Out.

The second step follows swiftly behind: we've got to solve the problem of inertia by getting into movement, but not just any movement. This is where you need to invest heavily into processes and *do the work*. This starts with mapping out where you need to head, getting real with progress, and putting dates, milestones and moments down on paper so that progress has a chance of happening. And always ensuring that the progress that we're making is still connected to a purpose that resonates with us—that there's a 'why' behind the 'what'. We do this by clearly setting out a map, your map. Your process isn't necessarily copied from someone else but is unique to you. This is your blueprint to come back to when you feel blindfolded by a lack of progress.

Getting found when we're feeling lost

With our smart phones at the ready and easy access to the interwebs at any given moment, we live in a time where physically getting lost is rarer than it used to be. In my childhood, I remember family trips on the back roads to 'Woop Woop' where we had really only two ways to find our direction. The first was having a map of the area (which we only very occasionally had), and the second involved asking a local person for directions. The second one was fraught with hurdles, from the quality of directions received from the local (go 400 metres, turn right ... no, no left, yeah left ... past the place where Barry hangs out his washing ... then follow your nose to the cedar tree ...), to the fact that Dad's internal 'hunter-gatherer-honing' pride made it impossible for him to actually ask the said local for directions in the first place (much to Mum's frustration). The result? Wrong turns, backtracking, hungry-whingy kids in the back seat, and silence between Mum and Dad. Not to mention the extra time and petrol required.

BUILD THE MAP THAT IS RIGHT FOR YOU AND IS BUILT ON YOUR VALUES.

Now these 'interesting' family road trips weren't all bad. We got to explore areas we'd never seen before, and Dad's look of pride and relief when we finally reached our destination was worth seeing. But having a map with us meant that, rather than something to endure, the explorations of back streets became intentional because we now knew how to get back on track. For you, in an era where time is precious and resources are finite, if you don't invest in processes and have a clear map for the landscape you want to explore, the casualty rate can be brutal. And the main casualties could be your dreams and desires. For me, these are too precious to risk on 'just winging it'.

Move away from feeling lost to feeling located. Think of this like the navigation on your maps app that brings up your 'little blue dot' to tell you where you are. At any point along the journey when you make a turn that doesn't quite land you at the place you thought it would, zoom back to your map and find your 'little blue dot'. Make sure you square away the time to focus on process. Build the map that is right for you and is built on your values. When you feel lost in the process, know that your 'little blue dot' will find you and help you decide what the next move should be.

Five essential components of maps

So building a process comes through action, and within this chapter ('Map it') and the next two ('Chunk it' and 'See it') you are going to have to do some work. What I recommend is that you make this fun. This is your time to get out of your head and get stuff onto paper, and the best resource you can invest in is some stationery that will bring your vision to life. If you're anything like me in a stationery store, you might just approach this as a 'one-of-everything' type of situation, but these are a few things that I'd recommend at a minimum:

» unruled art notebook in A3 size

» coloured pens

» whiteboard or vision board

» clear wall space you can put ideas and accountability actions on.

When we start to talk about mapping, we can identify five commonalities for any map. We're going to use these as guideposts to creating your map for moving forward. These five components are:

1. *title:* refers to everything the map covers

2. *orientation:* identifies which way is up

3. *legend:* highlights the symbols to use to interpret the map

4. *scale:* shows the perspective we're looking at

5. *date:* connects the map to the context.

We're going to use these components to create your blueprint.

1. TITLE

Set your title for this map, covering what the map is about. This title is your goal, clearly stated and specific. While this sounds like an obvious step, the truth is setting a clear goal can be harder than you first think.

You might have a vague idea about where you want to head, but have you actually articulated a clear goal? For example shift, 'I want to get fit' (vague), into something concrete like, 'I want to do a five kilometre run in October' (specific). Fear can hold you back from putting what's in your heart into words out into the world. What if others laugh? What if it doesn't come off?

This is the time to shut down those voices of doubt and write down your goal. Make it big. Make it real. Make it scare you a little bit.

Action:

» Open your art book to the first page and write down your goal.

2. ORIENTATION

The orientation on the map points us to true north, which, for this map, are your high priority values. These are your 'why', which sit behind what you are doing here and now. When you feel disconnected in your process, coming back to these values will reorientate you to what is important.

Action:

» Around your goal, write down your high priority values as they stand today.

» Get creative with the next few pages in your art book and dedicate one page per value. Write down things that help you connect back to these values, draw pictures and stick in images.

3. LEGEND

Typically a legend on a map defines any key symbols and markers along the way — for example, a black dot might be the symbol for a city with a population over one million. So the legend helps you to interpret the map and understand what you encounter along your route (and know essential things like where the closest toilets are).

When you think about mapping your goal, the legend highlights your key markers — those regular rituals that you want to build as you pursue this new direction. These are the rituals that will help you achieve your goal and they become the anchor you can come back to when busy shows up. For example, your rituals may be things like:

»   writing at a local coffee shop at 5 am each morning (my ritual for writing this book; yes, one was open)

»   setting exercise clothes out by your bedroom door the night before

»   having a 9 am Monday 'powwow' with the team

»   going for Friday arvo drinks with friends.

Action:

»   Write down three to five key rituals that you are going to commit to that will help you achieve your goal.

»   Slot these rituals into your calendar so they become part of your schedule.

4. SCALE

On a map, we want to understand the scale that we are looking at — think of the difference between the Google Earth view and the detail of the local cul-de-sac. In this case, the scale represents your current perspective of the sheer amount of space that is being considered.

Within psychology, getting people out of overwhelm often comes with changing the scale that they are currently viewing. Overwhelm often feels very close — we only look at today, tomorrow or next week — and when we think about the future it's tarred with the fear that next year will be exactly the same. We're unable to entertain thoughts of what might be different.

This is the time to entertain a different future, because we can't be what we can't see. If we want to win a new project with a client, we need to be able to see ourselves shaking the hand of the client, sealing the deal. If we want to take up running, we need to see ourselves crossing the finishing line of a five-kilometre race.

For your scale, consider how this change will have an impact on you in five weeks' time, five months' time, and five years' time.

Action:

» If you commit to this goal, write down what will you have achieved in:

  » five weeks' time

  » five months' time

  » five years' time (and it's totally okay to daydream and play with this).

» When you achieve these, how will you feel? Write down what you will be most proud of in:

  » five weeks' time

  » five months' time

  » five years' time (again, it's totally okay to daydream and play with this).

5. DATE

Maps are continually updated with additional information and improved accuracy as the details for the area shown increase. This is particularly the case when the landscape is continually changing. The reality is that the goals you had ten years ago were different from what you have now. Your goals in twelve months' time may also be significantly different.

Putting a date on your map gives you context. Plug into where you are right now in this point in your life. Set check-in and review dates to come back to your map. In the next chapter, 'Chunk it', we'll look specifically at having 90-day goals. This is the time and space to check in with your map, see where the landscape has changed, and update it with improved accuracy. You can also check in that it still aligns with your values, because these may shift.

Action:

» Go back to your goal page and write today's date on it.

» Schedule times in your calendar to check back in with your map in three months' time, and in six months' time.

Track the action that gets the traction

When it comes to mapping out the blueprint for your processes, knowing what you are tracking is important. Even more important is tracking the actions that give you the most traction. For example, certain conversations with the right people will move your project forward. Getting your product in the right store will open up a new wave of clientele. Get clear on what behaviours actually lead to progress.

In our business, we know that 'coffees = work' — meaning, us making the time to have coffees with clients, connectors and contacts invariably leads to work. Not every time, of course. (We always make sure the coffee we have is good, but even good coffee is not good enough to guarantee work 100 per cent of the time.) But in our business, we know this is the action that gives us the traction to keep growing.

GET CLEAR ON WHAT BEHAVIOURS
ACTUALLY LEAD TO PROGRESS.

When we get busy delivering and designing programs, the coffees start to drop off the weekly to-do list, our contacts start to diminish, and our sales funnel dries up. This, therefore, becomes a key action that we need to focus on even when we get busy. This is the metaphorical ball we can't afford to drop. When we don't pay attention to it, we pay for it.

Think about the action or actions that give you the best traction. Is it catching up with a certain friend who always leaves you inspired and energised? If so, schedule in a monthly lunch together rather than wait for a reason. Is it getting up by 5 am, because when you get up at that hour you exercise and the rest of your day is always better? If so, set that alarm, put out your exercise clothes and make sure it happens. And when these actions drop off the radar, as they will do during holiday times or when you're not well, then hit reset and schedule them back in again.

It's the tracking of these key actions you want to focus on.

Action:

» Write down the key targets or activities that will give you the most amount of traction.

Don't overthink it

We can all fall into the trap of thinking and overthinking, and this process can actually be not only a distraction habit but also a compulsion. Of all the things we can become addicted to, overthinking it is high on the list. We fear that if we don't think and obsess about it, we can't possibly get started, so we run through every step of the process, working through all of the things that need to get done.

You do have enough time. Consider the time you have available not just in chunks of days but even in terms of minutes. Ask yourself, 'Where am I going to allocate my minutes here? Map out your priorities and find the time — so you can say something like, 'I've got a big product I'm working on, I wish I had three weeks to deliver it, but over the next week if I do five hours that will get it sorted'. Paying attention to what is happening is key.

Get it out of your head. The key to this action is to physically map it out. Overwhelm grows in the dark, and it loves to be aloof. The moment we square overwhelm in the eye, really look at it and put what needs to be done under the microscope, it loses its stronghold on us. Then we can get to work, chunking out the work we need to do to start making progress.

Life hack: Hire accountability

Willpower is a limited resource and, while you might want something badly enough, the truth is the willpower it takes to stay the course can be depleted. This life hack can help.

The idea

Roy Baumeister is an American psychologist whose cookie research first highlighted the limited resource of willpower. This is why having a person in our corner is important — they keep us accountable when willpower has left the building.

Here are three sure-fire signs that it's time to hire external accountability:

1. Inner dialogue is mostly negative.

2. You've been through a period of inactivity.

3. You want to speed up the process (an external person can bring speed to the game).

The action

Research the experts, individuals and/or communities who can help you to stay the course in achieving your goal. Google them, chat with your contacts, and reach out on social media. Find the resources you have and then hire the accountability that you need.

Connect with individuals and communities who have a strong focus on progress and set up a system that holds accountability.

Remember: hiring accountability is not a sign of weakness; it's a sign that your goal is important and you want to give it the best shot of success.

CHAPTER 10
Chunk it

The cost of Freak Out is our sanity, because we feel like we're making millimetres of progress in a million different directions, but not going anywhere fast. This is where our friends are sick of hearing how we are going to save the world, and our teams play bingo on the number of motivational clichés we use and roll their eyes because really nothing has changed.

The thing that we hold dear — our gut instinct, our intuition — seems to be giving us the wrong message because nothing is happening, or certainly not happening the way that we had hoped it would.

After the last chapter, though, we've got a blueprint mapped out. You've incorporated the stuff that matters and the plan looks epic. It's amazing, your best work yet. The Freak Out has started to subside because now you have a clear direction and it looks doable — it's big, hard work, but still doable.

This is the danger zone that very few of us talk about. The reason it's a danger zone is because our anxiety has been significantly reduced by the planning. Working in clinical settings I would see this with individuals all the time. The anxiety and unrest prompted them to pick up the phone and make an appointment, and the need for things to change instigated them attending the appointment. The situation had become bad enough to be a catalyst for action. Do a good job as a psychologist of alleviating that anxiety, however, and the drive to get uncomfortable again is gone. We need to move out of this danger zone.

From idea to action

When we are in the midst of overwhelm, we often take time out to write ourselves a to-do list. Getting everything out of our head and down on paper means we now know what needs to get done — and we feel on top of it. But what do we then do? We pop the kettle on, cuddle up on the couch with a magazine, switch on our latest TV series, and promise ourselves we'll get round to the list later. Woah, there, buddy — don't be sitting back and celebrating that epic Gantt chart just yet.

This is the moment when we need to realise that having a grand plan isn't the end of the road. At some point we've actually got to *do the work*, and get into the grind of executing. And that's not as sexy as the planning. In fact, it can be downright boring. This stuff is hard. It takes resources and energy, and you might even get it wrong along the way.

Remember: perfection is not the goal, progress is. And when we explore neuroscience, we find that our brains are actually hardwired for progress. So let's make this internal drive work for us, rather than against us.

Harnessing dopamine

Dopamine is a neurochemical hormone associated with motivation, focus and mood, playing key roles in our habit formation, memory and many other high-order cognitive functions. Its most important job, though? Being our internal reward drug. You feel proud of finishing off something on your to-do list? Bam. Dopamine. Every time you take a step towards your goal, you get a dopamine hit. Take another step, you get another hit. It's what gets us off the couch, and taking action in the world.

The hormone is arguably the most addictive substance known to human beings. Individuals who have detoxed off chronic substance use will often feel a 'craving' long after the illicit drugs have left their systems — that's dopamine. Dopamine is the neurochemical response that sits behind our drive to play poker machines — because we don't know when the machine will 'pay out', when it does we get a hit of dopamine.

Do you ever feel like you can't be separated from your phone for an extended period of time? Do you constantly check for text messages, Facebook notifications, tweets? Do you find it impossible to ignore the 'ding' of an email? Dopamine is the reason. When your phone or computer 'pay out' via an email or text, you get a dopamine reward, and so you want to keep seeking this. This is why it's impossible to concentrate after you hear the 'ding' of a notification. Your brain is wired to check it out. You know that you get a hit of dopamine simply looking at your phone because of the seeking and reward you've previously experienced through this device. So if you want to ditch the distractions, turning your phone to silent won't work. You've got to physically leave it in another room.

Dopamine causes 'seeking' behaviour — that is, to want, desire and seek out, increasing goal-directed behaviour. Dopamine makes you curious about ideas and fuels your search for information. It's the reason that you jump on the internet for two minutes to grab a recipe for pancakes, and find yourself reading about Kim Kardashian's latest antics 40 minutes later. Dopamine is our 'wanting' chemical, and we generally seek more than we feel satisfied with.

Dopamine is a selfish chemical — hedonist-driven, it's all about getting things done now, focusing on short-term wins and not worrying about running over long-term goals in the process. But we can harness this chemical to our advantage if we engineer how we get things done. Dopamine increases when we're organised and finish tasks, regardless of the size of the task, regardless of the importance of the task. Physically checking something off a to-do list satisfies our brain.

Here are a few ways we can boost and harness the power of dopamine for good:

» *Get creative:* beautiful environments, coloured pens and good design will boost your motivation to do the work.

» *Movement:* taking the stairs or going for a walk in your lunch break boosts dopamine levels too — exercise doesn't have to be arduous in order to be effective. Get up from your desk and have a boogie! Factoring in movement breaks into your day will see you achieving more than slogging out back-to-back hours.

» *Music:* get into the zone of activity by putting on your fav grooves. Dopamine loves that stuff.

Harness the 'reward circuitry' in your brain by ditching the distractions of doing small tasks, and set up a system to be making progress in the directions that matter. Break down your map into chunks and you'll shift the big ideas into specific, tickable actions. And then you can soak up the dopamine that you'll get when you get stuff done.

HARNESS THE 'REWARD CIRCUITRY' IN YOUR BRAIN BY DITCHING THE DISTRACTIONS OF DOING SMALL TASKS, AND SET UP A SYSTEM TO BE MAKING PROGRESS IN THE DIRECTIONS THAT MATTER.

Work like a rock star

Don't you love the swagger of a front man? You'll remember I confessed in the introduction to this book to listening to Keith Urban. I'm not ashamed of this, either. Nor should I be. But I do have another confession to make on the music front.

My other confession is I've fallen under the spell of a few charismatic front men over the years. The 'noughties' saw me dreamy over Paul Dempsey from indie-band Something for Kate far too often. Before that, for the best part of the 1990s it was Eddie. Yep, Eddie Vedder — the legend of grunge metal and lead man for Seattle superstars Pearl Jam — had my heart. That growling voice. That angst and darkness. In retrospect, Eddie had a fair bit to do with me becoming a psychologist I think. I could've soothed his troubled soul.

And the 1980s. Of course, the '80s! As a teenager, I was completely obsessed with the powerfully masculine George Michael from Wham! (Ummm ... whoops!)

So, like many others, I've always had a fascination for the swagger of the rock star. And my latest fascination? Chris Martin from Coldplay. I've already raved about what an outstanding band they are. As the front man, Chris is a genius. To be fair, my and Chris's relationship (it's a relationship, right?) didn't start out as instant infatuation. Sure, I liked tracks like 'Yellow', off their first album *Parachutes*, but I'd always found him to be ... well, there's no kind way to put this ... a bit dweeby and introverted. He kinda reminded me of a kid I went to high school with who was the quiet music genius who kept to himself — and was the teenage epitome of uncool.

But in 2002 I found myself among 10 000 of my closest friends at the music festival Splendour in the Grass at Byron Bay. Daz and I squeezed our way forward in the crowd — never mind that we were the only people over 30 anywhere in the mosh pit — and waited for Coldplay to come out and close the two-day festival. To be honest, I was tired, my feet hurt and the human sardine can that had formed near the stage was hardly my idea of fun (I can hear you whispering, 'Ya old fart' from here), but Daz was a big fan and had been waiting to see them. And then Chris Martin walked out. And there's no polite way to say it: he fucking owned that stage.

Oh. My. God.

Literally. I mean, he was god-like. Powerful. Passionate. Possessed. And I was infatuated.

That's what rock stars do. They have the ability to — when the moment requires it — get into a state and just own it. And that's what we're going to do in this chapter; we're going to make you a rock star by breaking down your time and then every week programming a jukebox of hits for you so you can strut the stage rather than slink away when in Freak Out.

Break it down

In order to create a sense of momentum in your actions and to shift your ideas into concrete tasks, we need to break it down. For example, if you need to write a book, break it down into the chapters. To achieve a financial target at work, break it down into milestone targets.

Because every goal is different, here we're going to use the units that are most consistent for any idea, project or pursuit — that is, breaking it down into chunks of time.

The three main elements we're going to work with are:

» 90-day targets

» 30-day themes

» 7-day focus.

It's from these quarterly targets, monthly themes, and the weekly focus that our actions kick into gear. They cover the fun stuff, the boring stuff, and the stuff that just has to get done in order to get moving. Through these different time frames, you can make sure you're doing the work that will move you closer to your end goal.

90-DAY TARGETS

Chances are you'll have key things that you want to achieve over the year ahead. You might even have some New Year's resolutions that you have stuck with. The first chunk to focus on now in moving forward is setting your 90-day targets. Project yourself forward to the end of the coming quarter — what do you want to have finished?

Projects that matter

Peter Cook is an Australian thought leader who is obsessed with implementation and, in particular, he talks about creating projects that matter. These aren't just the work-type projects that get mandated to us by our organisations, or the home-type projects that involve doing the washing; these are projects that are important to you. They might be organising your photo collections, or they might be attending more networking events. What you could create a project around is unlimited — although the project needs to be specific enough for you to be able to say whether you have achieved it or not. For example, 'getting healthier' is hard to measure, but 'moving every day' is a project you can tick off.

Within your 90-day time frame, design no more than three primary projects that matter. Leo Babauta, founder of Zen Habits, purports if we have more than three main projects we are focusing on at once, we can get distracted from our goals. One of your three projects needs to be a personal project. (In his presentations, Cook tells the story of the personal project of asking his now-wife to marry him. It was an epic project that involved an interstate flight, friends and feasts.)

What are your three projects for the next 90 days?

Creating accountability

Chris Martin doesn't just sit back and write songs when he feels like it; he's got a team of people who hold him accountable to stepping up. You need to gather your people around you who do the same. Setting your projects is the start, and sticking to these requires a level of accountability. When it comes to focusing on the next 90-day projects, four levels of accountability are possible. Choose the one you are going to focus on in order to get the job done:

» *personal:* accountable to yourself (this takes some serious, no bull-shit pulling from you to work, though)

» *peer:* accountable to a friend (it's gotta be your 'you need to do this' friend, not your 'stuff it, let's head to the coast for the week' friend)

» *positional:* accountable to your boss, shareholders, stakeholders, kids (this is the big guns — if you've been around a three-year-old lately you'll know their memory of the promises you make are rock-solid)

» *public:* accountable to people within the general public (*#hashtagit*, track it; you never know who'll pull you back in line).

Who is going to keep you accountable?

30-DAY THEMES

Gretchen Rubin, *New York Times* best-selling author of *The Happiness Project*, committed to pursuing happiness through having a monthly focus. Each month she would focus on different aspects of exploring happiness, from getting more sleep and decluttering her home to building connections. In the same way, you can break down your 90-day projects into a 30-day theme. The start of each month gives you a fresh slate to step into.

Connect your themes to your 90-day projects. What do you need to step into more in order to turn these projects into a reality? Use your responses as ideas for your monthly theme.

Some of the key themes that might give you guidance are:

» movement

» connection

» curiosity

» rest

» play

» creativity

» nourishment

» presence

» connection

» gratitude

» rest

» surprises

» processes.

What theme are you (or your team) going to step into for the next 30 days?

7-DAY FOCUS (THE 10 HOURS THAT MATTER)

When it comes to shifting into action, your focus isn't on cramming more into your day. If you're a person who needs 10 hours of sleep per night, then get it. I'm not going to say, 'Suck it up, sleeping's for when you're dead'. What I will say, though, is maximise and prioritise ten key hours in your week, and use this time wisely.

During these ten focused, waking hours, you can make a fundamental difference to your entire life. What sort of difference they make is all about how you program these ten hours.

To clarify, I don't mean you need to program your entire week, minute by minute. What I'm talking about is being super smart in programming these ten focused hours. Like a jukebox, you get to program what goes in, so that you enjoy what comes out. If you don't program this time, you'll be left listening to Kenny Rogers on replay. Honestly, if you give me ten hours of your best, it will change your life.

Once you have these ten hours, you can then divide them up into three different areas, specifically 5 + 3 + 2:

» 5 × 'rock and roll' hours every week

» 3 × 'alternative listening' hours every week

» 2 × 'easy listening' hours every week.

Let's explore these three areas in more detail.

Rock and roll: 5 hours

The first five hours to schedule into your calendar each week are your 'rock and roll' hours. This is time for pedal to the metal, all effort in, mass productivity time. This time is about getting rid of distractions and just getting stuff done. These are five times one-hour slots throughout your week that you will dedicate to getting stuff done. Aligning these hours to the times when you are most alert and awake will ensure that your biology is on your side too.

At the start of your week spend time going over your calendar and schedule in these rock and roll hours. The reason to do this on a weekly basis is that it's likely that every week is different. Shift and schedule this time around meetings and other commitments.

Now some of you might be thinking, *Five hours a week is not much for productivity. I've got a tonne more stuff to get done.* But have a think about professional sporting teams, such as those in the AFL (Australian Football League) that we have here in Australia. Players in the AFL teams are professionals whose full-time job is to play the game. The reality is, though, while their full-time job is football, the 'business end' is actually only about two hours a week, for about 22 weeks of the year, sometimes 26 (depending on whether they get into the finals and how successful they are). The same goes for you and these five hours. This is 'game day' time, so deep dive into the work that shifts and makes a difference. The rest of your week is for planning, strategy, meetings, connecting.

The following are key tips to help get the most out of these rock and roll hours:

» *Shut your damn door:* get rid of all the distractions. If you're a boss or manager and you've got an open door policy, it's very likely your day is filled with interruptions. Remember: it's only five hours a week, so let people know and shut the door. They can come flooding back in when you're done. Get the most out of that hour, and it will repay back to your team tenfold in terms of you being able to be completely present with them when you are connecting and talking with them, because you know that what you needed to get done has been done.

» *Leave your phone behind:* if you work in an open-plan office or you can't shut the door, often you need to find another space for these rock and roll hours, but you know what happens when you leave the office, right? People ring you to find out where you are. Divert your phone, leave your phone behind, let people know, go somewhere else, and do what needs to be done. Sometimes your mass productivity, your rock and roll hours, are actually networking or connecting with people. This rule still applies. Give them your full attention. Don't have your phone as a distraction and a reminder of what else is waiting back at the office. Just leave your phone behind.

» *Set a clear time frame:* make the time you schedule in no less than half-hour blocks because you need at least this length of time to get immersed in an activity. For me, I prefer one-hour blocks. Set the clock, stay to the end. Then the full time you've allocated is a race and a frenzy — you're not fluffing around for the first ten minutes, or being proud of yourself for what you've achieved for the last ten minutes. If you've allocated an hour, maximise the full 60 minutes; once the 60 minutes is up, step away.

» *Reward yourself:* what the research tells us about how habits are formed is that a habit becomes ingrained when we get a reward at the end. You need to have a solid transition and a solid break. It might even be for a couple of minutes, but go and grab a coffee, go for a quick walk around the office, or duck outside for a moment. Create a break and a reward for yourself.

The next block of time you need to schedule in is creating space to think differently — your 'alternative listening' hours.

Alternative listening: 3 hours

Your 'alternative listening' time is three hours in your week where you explore alternative ways and perspectives. The idea here is a bit like a professional swimmer who does yoga as an alternative training, or an athlete who cross-trains in a totally different field. It's about you thinking about alternative channels and different perspectives on the work that you need to do.

One of the biggest gripes I hear people say is, 'I just don't have time to work *on* my business because I'm so busy working *in* it'. This is similar to, as a manager, hearing people say, 'Look, I don't have time to work on culture or how my team get along because we've just got stuff that we have to do'. You need to make time for that stuff, and you need to square it away because people won't hand it to you. (Your boss isn't likely to come to you and say, 'Hey, how about you just take an hour to go and think about how you're doing your job or how we could do it better'.)

Here are a few ideas for places to explore new ways of thinking:

» *TED Talks:* 20-minute presentations from experts and thought leaders from around the world on various topics and the latest research.

» *Podcasts:* check out the top podcasts on iTunes in various categories. For me, Jonathan Fields' Good Life Project is my go-to podcast. *#brilliant*

» *Slow thinking time*: clarity requires space, so give yourself enough time for ideas to bubble up.

» *Play 'Apples and Oranges'*: this is an activity that was shared by great friends of ours, design experts from Jaxzyn Design, Jen and Dougal Jackson. The goal is to compare an industry different from the one you are in and look at what they do that you could incorporate into your world. In a work context, you might say to your team, 'This time we're going to look at the hospitality industry,' and they then have a week to investigate and acquire ideas themselves, after which you come together for a lunch and talk about what people have uncovered and what they think that industry does really well that could put into place with your team.

Easy listening: 2 hours

The two 'easy listening' hours each week are for active, planned relaxation. This is actually about creating white space in your week, because really, how often do we have it?

We never do. We jump in the car and we're either on the phone or we're listening to the radio. We're constantly in contact with people from the moment we wake up to the moment we fall into bed.

So here are the rules for your easy listening hours:

1. *They need to not be part of your regular routine.* If you normally get up and go for a walk in the morning, these hours are not part of that. If you normally go to yoga on a Wednesday afternoon, they're not part of that either.

2. *Vigorous exercise doesn't count.* I know that may sound kind of counterintuitive, because you might go, 'Look, that's my "me-time". That's my complete downtime'. But research shows that the hormones produced when we're doing vigorous exercise, although great for our body and our mind in a whole range of different ways, aren't about providing downtime. You might get some great ideas when you're doing exercise (I know I do) but you're not experiencing downtime for your body or your brain.

3. *You should feel energised and refreshed.* After these hours you should feel like you've had a massive night's sleep, and recharged and ready to get back into it.

4. *They should be tech-free.* Leave the devices behind so you can quiet the mind.

Remember: your rock and roll hours are your peak hours. They are the time to rip in, no excuses. It's not about the number of hours, but how you use these hours.

When it comes to the alternative hours, ditch the distractions — just get rid of them.

When it comes to the easy listening hours, create white space to hear nothing, to just chill out and be in the downtime.

For all of the hours in your jukebox, focus is the key, and being the watchdog of your time is critical. Avoid the trap of cluttering up your calendar with commitments that derail your focus. Carve out the time to get the key actions done in order to make progress.

Decision-making

You are a decision-making machine — literally and metaphorically. The ability of human beings to discern information quickly, filter out the irrelevant data and grasp onto what is relevant in this given circumstance to make a call is unsurpassed. All of that happens in the nanosecond that you reach for the choc-chip muffin and cup of tea. You are an expert at decision-making.

Where things start to go haywire, however, is when we throw cognitive load into the mix and decision-fatigue kicks in. Pay attention to the little decisions every day that you don't need to be making, and remove decision-fatigue by getting streamlined in your processes. Consider the following:

» Wear a similar outfit for similar tasks.

» Have the same lunch on the same days — we have 'sushi Monday' in our team.

» Park in the same area at the shopping centre.

» Put your clothes out the night before.

» Check emails only at certain times throughout the day.

Reducing the cognitive load by removing these small decisions means you can focus on the more important decisions, and start seeing your progress.

Life hack: The 15-minute rule

To combat inertia we need to create momentum — this life hack shows you how.

The idea

We are completion beings, and when we start something we are eager to finish it. Not sure if this is true? Ask a child to stop playing their game on the iPad and their response will be 'I just have to finish [insert mission]'. The problem is that these games are engineered never to be finished. Hence the tantrum that follows when the inevitable happens and you take the iPad off them. But we can take advantage of our own urge for completion. Commit to getting started and see where it leads you.

The action

Commit to fifteen uninterrupted minutes on a task — whatever the task, you have to stick with it for fifteen minutes. If at the fifteen-minute mark you're done, get up and go do something else. Often what happens, though, is that we're absorbed into the process and have started making progress. So we stick with it till we finish the next chunk.

The kicker, though, is that if you get distracted or your focus shifts onto social media, emails or something else, you need to start your fifteen minutes again.

CHAPTER 11
See it

Johann Sebastian Bach was a prolific composer in his time. While his work may not be on your daily Spotify list, chances are you've heard it at some point. Over his extensive career, how many concertos do you think Bach wrote? Rather than come up with a specific number, choose a range where you feel 98 per cent confident that you're on the money — for example, you might say between 100 and 500 concertos.

Psychologists Howard Raifa and Marc Alpert have asked hundreds of people this question (among other questions), asking them to rate their knowledge within a strong band of confidence. Their research focused on exploring the gap between what people confidently affirmed that they knew and what they actually knew. Their results were fascinating: instead of 2 per cent of respondents being wrong (which would fit in with them feeling 98 per cent confident), they found that 40 per cent of their respondents proved incorrect with the range they provided. In other words, they overestimated their confidence in their knowledge. (In regards to Bach, for example, over his total output of more than 1100 compositions, only 28 are classed as concertos. That fact will totally come in handy at your next trivia night event.) Raifa and Alpert named this phenomenon the 'overconfidence effect'.

We apply this effect in many aspects of our lives — from overconfidence in the stock market and the property market, to overconfidence in our ability to be safe drivers (it's always the other idiots on the road that make it unsafe). Interestingly enough, experts suffer from the overconfidence effect more than others — an economist will not be able to predict the price of oil in five years' time any better than a zookeeper, for example, but they will state their prediction with confidence. Overconfidence kicks into not only our ability to predict but also our ability overall. For example, in his book *The Black Swan*, philosopher and statistician Nicholas Taleb found that 84 per cent of Frenchmen estimate that they are above average lovers. Obviously, 'above average' means only 50 per cent should rate themselves in this category, but the confidence and swagger of Frenchmen is clearly high.

Each of us wears the badge of overconfidence, and one of the things that we are notoriously bad at predicting is how long things actually take to get finished. Progress is halted when the overconfidence effect kicks in. The reality is that we overestimate our ability and skills and grossly underestimate how long it takes to get the job done. Ever needed to push back a deadline? Then you've fallen into this trap. Renovations are notoriously known for blowing out, both in budget and time frames — our overconfidence of the task and underestimation of the true length of time required kicking in again.

But we do this all the time, don't we? 'Yep, I'll declutter the house, make hats for the kids' Easter hat parade, take on a new project at work, commit to running a five-kilometre race in two weeks' time, and write a book, all in the next week. Sure thing. I'M ALL OVER IT.'[1] And, progress, the poor thing, gets death-ridden from the outset. No wonder Freak Out is what turns up when this is the schedule we give progress. In order

---

1   Exact excerpt from my internal dialogue

to shift out from the shadows of over-commitment, progress needs to become visible.

From hidden to visible

Our internal measure of progress is flawed and can't be relied upon. When we trust what's happening inside, we don't always see the progress that we make, and we miss seeing when progress starts to slip. We need to get outside ourselves and find a way to shift to an external way of tracking progress, turning it from hidden to visible. We need to get honest with both our abilities (and how we sabotage our own progress) and the true length of a project. We need to eyeball progress. Literally *see it*. Shift progress from being a hidden measure, to being something that we see on a regular basis.

This process starts with us getting real about the ways that we self-sabotage our own progress. In particular, we need to understand the four archenemies of progress, each of which we engage in from time to time.

The four archenemies of progress (and their antidotes)

The world is a busy place, with plenty of obstacles between us and achieving success. Yet many of us also step into behaviours that sabotage our own progress and productivity — actually, not just many of us; all of us. Each and every one of us has fallen into these patterns of behaviour from time to time.

Sometimes we are conscious of what we are doing, but other times we unconsciously step into old habits that don't serve us very well.

Dr Jason Fox is the best-selling author of *The Game Changer* and *How to Lead a Quest*, working with Fortune 500 companies around motivation design. Dr Fox's research and thinking on the integral importance of progress in motivation, and how we need to design work to maximise the motivation of discretionary effort is world class.[2] He's also the greatest red-bearded man I know. Building on Dr Fox's research on the ways that we self-sabotage our own progress, he and I collaborated and identified the four archenemies of epic progress. These are the four ways that we consistently get in our own way when it comes to making progress. These are the four Ps:

>> perfectionism

>> procrastination

>> pessimism

>> people-pleasing.

While you will have dabbled in all of them, generally one or two will be your default way of operating. Let's get to know these four a little better and look at ways that we can finally step out of our own way and unfold a pathway for greater pro gress and success.

PERFECTIONISM

Perfectionism is not the same as having a high standard or striving for excellence. There is such a thing as healthy striving — it's that thing that pushes us to work harder, to pick up the phone one more time, and to push the boundaries.

Perfectionism, on the other hand, is the result of setting high and impossible standards, and at its core is the self-destructive belief system that our self-worth is attached to achieving these impossible standards. According to Dr Brené Brown, perfectionism is fuelled by the primary thought that, *If I look perfect and do everything perfectly, I can avoid or minimise the painful feelings of shame, judgement and blame.*

---

2   Go to www.drjasonfox.com for all the Foxy love you need. He is a genius.

The perfectionism mantra is 'There's never enough time'.

Why do we use it?

Perfectionism is a false shield. We use it because we believe it can protect us from feeling shame, or from being judged by others ('If I did it perfectly, they'd have nothing to judge').

Perfectionism perpetuates itself too. If we do experience judgement from others, we believe it's because we didn't work hard enough.

How does it hold us back?

Perfectionism steals our time and our headspace, consumes us with worry, and also robs the people around us of our work (particularly if we wait for it to be perfect before we show it to anyone). It robs us of progress and can get a project bogged down quicker than a sedan in the Sahara Desert.

PROCRASTINATION

Procrastination is putting something off that we know we should be doing. It's the irrational delay of something for no good reason, and often when action would have been preferable.

Procrastination is not always about inaction, however. In fact, the most common form of procrastination on a task in our busy world is by being too busy to do it. We distract ourselves with little tasks and avoid the important things we ought to be focusing on.

The procrastination mantra is 'I work better under pressure'.

Why do we use it?

We use it because often other tasks that are not as urgent actually give us a greater sense of progress than the very thing we ought to be focusing on.

The other reason we use it is because very occasionally procrastination pays off for us. The thing that you hadn't gotten around to doing is no longer needed or, better still, someone else has done it so you no longer need to.

How does it hold us back?

Procrastination often partners up with indecision and anxiety and can leave us feeling paralysed about a direction. It stops progress in its tracks because, well, nothing's really getting done.

PESSIMISM

You may have heard the saying, 'I'm not a pessimist; I'm a realist'. This is a nonsensical statement, because both optimists and pessimists can take a realistic view of a given situation; the difference is in how they deal with the reality they perceive.

Pessimism is the tendency to see the worst aspects of things and events. According to American psychologist Martin Seligman, pessimism is a way of seeing problems as permanent and pervasive — that they are never going to change, and this is going to affect everything. Pessimism is also the belief that my behaviour doesn't matter, and that I can't have any impact on changing what is happening.

The pessimism mantra is 'I'm just playing devil's advocate'.

Why do we use it?

Pessimism is a way of trying to protect ourselves by beating disappointment to the punch by expecting it. The problem is that it doesn't work. If we expect disappointment and then receive it, we're actually doubly-disappointed. On the other hand, if we expect the worst and things go well, we assume it's just a fluke and wait for something bad to happen. Or things never go as well as they could (more disappointment).

How does it hold us back?

When we are in a headspace of expecting less than great outcomes, often we find the cracks around us. A victim mentality and a learnt helplessness come with pessimism.

Pessimism also blocks our belief that our behaviours can actually have any impact on the situation. More often than not, we actually have more power in the overall outcome than we know.

PEOPLE-PLEASING

People-pleasing, at its core, is a noble venture, starting out from the inherent belief that we are here to serve and support others. This approach is needed in our workplaces more often, but our reasons for helping people can move it along the continuum to being dysfunctional.

If our reason for people-pleasing is a strong desire to be liked, validated and accepted by others, we move into overcommitting ourselves — and even potentially resenting the very people we want to be serving more. People-pleasing is when we let other people's priorities replace our own, committing to so many things that we are stretched too thin.

The people-pleasing mantra is, 'I have so much on my plate right now'.

Why do we use it?

Socially, a lot of self-reinforcement and validation comes from being the 'go-to' person — the one others can rely on to say yes and help out when things are busy. Sometimes, we even get recognised and rewarded for it by others.

Potentially letting people down is tough, so we'd rather suck it up and get on with it than rock the boat.

How does it hold us back?

It can feel hard to fault people-pleasing but this tendency is the slow sabotage. It can eat away at the quality of our work because we are stretched so thin we can't give anything the time and energy it truly deserves. It also takes us away from the activities and people who really matter to us.

THE ANTIDOTES

Each of these archenemies has an antidote that we can apply in order to step back into progress. Apply these antidotes liberally and get yourself moving again.

Perfectionism antidote

The challenge here is to get real about what factors are essential and what are superfluous. Employ the 80 per cent rule: get a task to 80 per cent and then either ship it or check in with others. If you find yourself spending way too long writing emails to stakeholders, for example, write your draft, get it to what you see as 80 per cent and then check in. You may find that your 80 per cent is completely fine and then you can move on.

Procrastination antidote

When your tendency is to put things off, wait till you have more information or leave a decision till later, know that chances are you've already got the information you need to make a reasonable decision. The antidote requires you to get into action, and schedule in an 'hour of power'.

Set yourself an hour for a full productivity blitz, and rip into the thing that you are putting off. Look it square in the face and wrestle with it for an hour. Often, within 40 minutes you will already feel more on top of what you need to do.

Pessimism antidote

The antidote for pessimism is simple and incredibly effective, but committing to it is hard. The antidote for pessimism is gratitude, because it's impossible to be pessimistic and grateful at the same time.

Write down something that you are grateful for here and now. Take the time to say thanks to a family member, a colleague, or your local barista. If pessimism still rears its head, apply gratitude in a higher dose until symptoms subside.

People-pleasing antidote

This antidote will result in having the true people-pleasers stop breathing. But stick with me because this antidote will change your world. Here it is: say no graciously. (And now breathe ...)

I get it; saying no is tricky. Saying no to a friend is really tricky. But remember that the goal is to make progress, and if you keep piling up your to-do list, progress is going to leave the building. You can be honest about saying, 'I want to give this my full attention and I can't right now'.

It's also important to say no when what you're being asked to do is not aligned with your values. Just because you can say yes doesn't mean you should. I've had to learn how to say no graciously, particularly if I can't see a compelling reason (or so I think) to say no. One area where I've had to learn this is when I'm being asked to speak at an event. When these requests first started coming in, the only question I used to ask was, 'Am I available?' If I was, I'd do it; if I wasn't, I wouldn't. Now I have a barrage of questions: Am I available? Does this excite me? Where would the time spent preparing, travelling and delivering this be better used? Is something else more important? Does this align with my goals?

If the speaking engagement isn't the best use of my time at that point, or doesn't align with my goals, I've had to learn how to say no graciously.

The following are three keys to keep in mind for your gracious 'no':

» *Find the gratitude:* outline that you are grateful for being asked, and honoured that you were thought of.

» *Actually say 'no' (or something equally as definitive):* 'I'll see' is not a no. 'Let me get back to you' is not a no. Don't hint or hope they understand. Instead, say

'I don't have the time for that at the moment'. Make it clear.

» *Offer to support in other ways:* only make this offer if these feel okay to you, and be careful of shifting the load to something else.

Let's get visual

Being able to visualise progress not only counteracts the overconfidence effect but also drives motivation. When we see where we are, we want to keep moving forward. Ticking off tasks on our to-do list is a way of visually tracking progress. Something inside of us wants to see the full list ticked off and we'll keep working until we do. (Or we'll sneakily write a new list and just transfer what we haven't gotten around to yet to tomorrow's list. Yep, I know your tricks!)

**WHEN WE SEE WHERE WE ARE,
WE WANT TO KEEP MOVING FORWARD.**

There are great examples of how we already visualise progress in our world. In a fundraising setting, we often see the thermometer as a visual tracking device. In a workplace setting, we use whiteboards, Gantt charts and reports to see progress. They may not be the best methods to use, however; they are often not well designed (they're so boring to look at) and often track the outcome rather than the effort. We see the business income rather than the number of coffees we've had with clients, for example. And these are one-way communication rather than something that individuals can interact with.

As you set up how you visualise the progress towards your goal, stick with the following three rules:

1. *Track the effort rather than the outcome:* in chapter 9 we spoke about tracking the action that makes a difference. In our business, for example, coffees = work.

While the outcome of securing work is reliant on an array of things, many outside of our control, the thing we have 100 per cent control over is catching up with people for coffees. When we visualise the effort that we control, motivation follows.

2. *Invest in good design:* you have full permission to go and spend a ridiculous amount of money on journals, whiteboards, pens, magnets, and even designers. Battle the boring and the beige and make your visual tracking something that brings joy when you see it, and something that you and others will want to engage with more.

3. *Make it interactive:* the nature of progress is that it's ever-changing. In a rapidly changing work environment, this progress can shift on a daily basis. Therefore, the way that we visualise progress needs to be dynamic and interactive so that we can engage with its evolution. Printing off an Excel spreadsheet and putting it on the wall won't cut it. Think magnets as markers, whiteboards that can be updated easily, or Advent calendar–style walls that have hidden chocolates when you unlock the next level.

THE COMPOUNDING EFFECT

When we see something over a period of time, it becomes the trophy of effort that we can be proud of. Use this compounding effect of visualising back-to-back effort to keep you moving towards your goal.

You can use this compounding effect in two ways:

» *Start streaking:* visually seeing a streak of the behaviour you are focusing on is a powerful way to increase dopamine levels. Seeing how many days in a row you've achieved something, for example, is motivating. Invest in a streaking calendar (no, not the kind that you used to see at the footy) and start ticking that stuff off.

> » *Focus on the trend, not the number:* the stock market is continually focusing more on trend lines than the daily numbers. The same is true when our goal is weight loss, where the reality is that weight fluctuations can be based on everything from dehydration to salt levels to the moon cycle. We can get deflated if we only concentrate on the single digit, whereas the overall trend may be more positive. When the individual figure can fluctuate, find a way to focus on the trend instead.

SET UP THE ENVIRONMENT

We are the product of our environment. If we see mess and chaos around us, we will feel messy and out of control. I'm not saying you can't do productive and hard work in a messy environment, but the length of time needed for you to get up to speed is longer. Getting into that state takes longer and you can't hit the ground running. Time is precious, remember — any hacks that we can put into place to engineer the environment for success is going to serve us in the long term.

SEE IT. DO IT. WATCH IT GROW

To help with motivation and progress towards your goal, you can go visual in three main places:

1. In physical and tactile areas at home or at work; for example, on:

   » the wall

   » butcher's paper

   » a whiteboard

   » sticky notes.

   Say your goal is to declutter the house, for example. You could get a floor plan of the house and put a star or sticker on areas as you do them. If your goal is to get into running, you could draw some foot shapes and, each time you go for a run, write down on them where you went, how far you ran and who you went with, and put them on a spare wall.

2. On your desktop; for example:

» online programs, such as project management software (for example, Basecamp)

» calendars

» a beautifully designed Excel spreadsheet.

3. In your back pocket (your smart phone, that is); for example:

» tracking apps such as MyFitnessPal, budgeting apps and Habit Streaks — all great ways to carry your motivation and tracking with you

» sharing on social media — looking through an Instagram account could be a way of visually seeing change and evolution.

Doing it anyway

One morning I asked my seven-year-old son to go and brush his teeth. (I love that this request always comes as a surprise, even though I ask him every single morning and every single night!) My son's response surprised me (okay, maybe it didn't but his actual words struck me). He turned to me, looked me square in the eye and, in a genuine and gentle manner, simply said, 'No, I don't feel like it'.

It had never occurred to me that you could be in a mood to not want to brush your teeth. Being bored, angry, frustrated or love-struck, or even wanting to daydream — I didn't think any of these were really a tipping point to prevent us from brushing our teeth. Regardless of how you are feeling, you go through the motions — because, well, it's kinda gross if you don't.

Then why do we apply this 'regardless of how you feel you do it anyway' rule to shining the pearly whites, but we don't apply it to other behaviours that are equally important for us to do each day? For example:

1. We skip exercise, because we're not in the mood.
2. We avoid important conversations, because we're waiting to feel bulletproof.
3. We don't get around to starting that new project, because we're not ready yet.

When we don't have the energy to do what matters, we assume we're not 'meant to'.

When it comes to tripping up progress nothing does it better than our own heads. Our self-doubt and fear of uncertainty kick in and we are left feeling lost and blindfolded, unsure of what move we should be making next. Facing these fears and increasing our tolerance for uncertainty has a way of shifting our mindset towards making progress.

Life hack: Brainstorm ways to get visual

Here's a life hack to help you visualise the progress that's important for you.

The idea

We can get stuck into the habit of doing what we've always done. Taking the time to let your brain run free and explore other ways of visualising progress can help you move towards your goals.

The action

Examples of how we can visualise progress are numerous in our world, from the well-used charity thermometer image, to a project Gannt chart. More dynamic examples are rich in our technological world, from being able to track the Uber car you've just booked, to being able to see the likes on your latest Instagram masterpiece going up.

The key is to tap into these examples that are currently in your world and explore creative and new ways you can visualise the steps that matter for you. Arrange a coffee date with your creative friend, team, or even with your cat. Throw around ways that you could creatively visualise progress towards your goal. Have fun. If your goal is to go for a walk every day, take a photo ever time you go for a walk, print these off and display them on a wall to see your progress.

Once you have a few ideas, choose one and then tweak as required.

Freak out wrap up

When it comes to setting up processes that will drive real progress — and so shift from blindfolded to having a blueprint, from idea to action, and from having your progress hidden to making it visible — come back to these three key actions:

1. *Map it:* values are clear but progress is not. Take the time to map out your goals, set in motion the rituals, schedule in your review dates, and get clear about the actions that get the traction for progress.

2. *Chunk it:* get out of the inertia that can happen when you've got an initial plan. Chunk down your time into 90-day targets and 30-day themes, and then focus on the 10 hours that matter every week. Do this and your inner rock star will shine.

3. *See it:* unless we make progress visible we can never be certain we've made it, and we've got no check-in to jolt us when we haven't. Start by combatting the four archenemies of progress: perfectionism, procrastination, pessimism and people-pleasing. Then get progress up so you can see it, maintaining the motivation of momentum.

Part V
Embrace
stand out

We have the greatest accountants in the world. Seriously — I never knew you could actually love your accountant, but Darren and I genuinely love our accountants. It's weird, right? But true. And the highlight of our quarterly meetings is the 'bouncing balls' — an animated graph where balls bounce around a quadrant model and then land on the quadrant that depicts the current financial health of our business. We're always cheering when it lands in the top right quadrant.[1] Because, as we all know, when it comes to quadrant models, the top right box is the one you want to be in. When you land there, you know all the work you've put in has paid off.

The same is true for the Stand Out model. When we are clear on our 'why' and we're making progress, our hard work means we can celebrate bouncing into the Stand Out quadrant. Perhaps a part of us believes when we hit this quadrant, the heavens will open up, the choir will kick into gear, and there'll be double rainbows all the way. Time to put your feet up; the hard work is done. Isn't it?

Sorry. But no. This is where the real work starts.

In fact, this is where the hardest work kicks into gear; the only real guarantee is that standing out will cost you your old identity. While shifting into Stand Out is aspirational (and a more desirable state than Check Out, Burn Out or Freak Out), to believe that's the end of the journey is to give yourself false hope. Success has knobs on it, and regardless of how awesome things are, they are never quite what you expected. You'll still have doubts, you'll still have heartache, things will still fall into a heap, and at times you'll not realise you've been wearing your shirt inside out for the entire day.

---

1   Yep, there are literally high fives and loud cheers. Plus the action replay as we call to see it again. And again.

In order to stay in this quadrant, and to transition through the cost of letting go of your old identity and having the capacity to truly invest in others, you need to focus on three key actions: being present, doing it your way and gathering your tribe. These actions are unpacked in the next three chapters.

CHAPTER 12
Be present

Shifting into Stand Out is exciting. This is the place where clarity of purpose waltzes with the type of progress that even freshly lit fireworks on New Year's Eve would be proud of. This is where things are happening, cool things — the kinda stuff your Facebook status was born for. Sounds like nirvana, doesn't it?

The reality is that, among the glow, there is also a mess that comes with success. A flipside that if we don't take the time to talk about has the potential to knock you down and leave you feeling winded, gasping for breath and questioning your decisions. Early on in this research a close friend asked me an interesting question — actually one that stopped me in my tracks. *Do people really want to Stand Out?* she questioned. And I get it. The tall poppy syndrome of wanting to cut down those who stick their neck out is alive and well. Why would we put ourselves out there for judgement and critique voluntarily?? Aren't we just big-noting ourselves; being a bit showy? To me living a Stand Out life isn't about fame or fortune. Becoming a celebrity is not necessarily the goal. To be honest, the pursuit of fame for fame's sake often requires the sacrifice of becoming something that you're not. That's the fast road to plunging into Check Out if ever I heard of one.

Living a Stand Out life is about shaking off the weight of expectation and stepping into who you are. Fully present. Fully you. Warts and all. And when you do, the test is to be here and experience both the highs and the uncomfortable lows. Being present to all of it is the toughest and most important action you can take.

The following sentiment has often been attributed online to the poet Charles Bukowski. Although no proof exists he ever said it, the notion sums up what opening the door to Stand Out can feel like:

Find what you love ... (Check!)

... and let it kill you. (Whoa, wait ... what???)

These words are urging us to Stand Out — and that starts with being present. Sitting in the mess of success is the hardest and most exhilarating thing we can do. Don't short-change yourself from this experience.

From blindsided to bold

When it comes to weddings and babies, everyone's got an opinion and they're not afraid to voice it. A week before our wedding, one piece of advice stuck with me because it was profoundly powerful. A friend from my work sat me down and said, 'When it comes to your day, don't forget to stop and soak up the moments. It'll be over in a flash, and if you don't pause, pay attention and breathe it in, you'll miss it'. I'm forever grateful for this advice — and grateful that it was followed by one of those even rarer moments when we actually listened to good advice. Our day was more magical, more meaningful and more 'whole' because of the act of noticing. And this act is not just about noticing the good or great moments but is also about noticing the moments where disappointment makes an entrance. Don't get me wrong — we soaked up the ceremony, we soaked up the photos with the family, and we also noticed and gave voice to our disappointment when it started raining during the reception (we had specifically sent an order in for zero rain). We paid attention in the moments when a wave of relief and exhaustion hit us; we paid attention to the sadness about missing friends who couldn't join us for the day.

Being present isn't just about noticing the good stuff and filtering out the rest. It's noticing it all, even the disappointing mess. It's in this way that we ensure that we aren't blindsided by the mess of success. In fact, stopping and being present to the disappointing mess is the most profound, important and bold thing we can do as we start to step into our new identity of living a Stand Out life. Boldness holds bravery and courage in the face of uncertainty. In fact, the only certainty in Stand Out is that success comes with conditions we weren't aware of. Boldness is the antidote.

Success has knobs on it

Anyone who has achieved a worthwhile goal knows that success, while amazing and exhilarating, is not necessarily smooth sailing. It's the person who completes their first marathon and then spends the next week living in fear of having to walk up any stairs they may have to encounter. It's the Olympic gold medal winner who's thrown into the spotlight of 3 am breakfast radio and TV, along with social media scrutiny moments after their win. And it's the business that grows rapidly, is wildly successful and still has to deal with a cashflow crisis while waiting for outstanding invoices to be paid.

So if you were expecting success to be plain sailing, you're in for a shock that will blindside you quicker than supermarkets selling hot cross buns on Boxing Day. Success has knobs on it, and sometimes those knobs are spiky and downright painful. However, these knobs and costs start to shift and shape our new identity as someone who can face the challenges that arise when we combine purpose and progress. As the challenges arise, so does the opportunity for growth.

With stepping into Stand Out comes responsibility. A biblical passage referred to throughout history by various people (from Voltaire to Winston Churchill) suggests that 'to whom much has been given, much will be demanded'. Or as the modern philosopher Spiderman would say, 'With great power there must also come great responsibility'. The more you step into the path you want to be following, the more you'll be asked to take on even greater challenges.

IDENTITY EXPANSION

The cost of stepping into Stand Out is our old identity, and this is a scary cost. Reshaping your identity shifts the sands that your belonging and connection are built on. If you've been the person who has always said yes, for example, and now you are setting up strong boundaries and saying no, your identity will change. And one thing that is guaranteed of this change is that there will be push back — sometimes from the very people who you were looking to support you.

Many have arrived at this place, not liked what was being served up for dinner and darted promptly back to Freak Out, Burn Out or Check Out to stay. Because even though the cost in these states is to our sanity, health or happiness, at least we know where we stand. Staying in Stand Out is a bold and courageous move and requires the internal work of expanding into the next evolution of your identity. What I love about this, though, is that, possibly for the first time ever, you have the chance to be strategic about what that identity evolution is. You're the artist at the crafting table, sculpting and moulding the features that align and work for you.

Your identity is a construct that started to form the moment you were born, and it continues to shift and re-shape itself until your final day. It is part protection mechanism and part bonding tool, and has a major role to play in the upkeep of our self-esteem and wellbeing. In fact, actively working on shaping our identity is a wellbeing process practised by just about every culture on the planet. So the big question remains: How often do you actively work on your identity?

TODAY'S BUSYNESS PALES IN COMPARISON TO TOMORROW'S IMPORTANT.

Too often we find ourselves working on 'work'. And nothing is wrong with that at the surface level; being busy has a type of nobility attached to it. But today's busyness pales in comparison to tomorrow's important. To believe that evolving our identity is possible, we need to first embody a growth mindset.

ADOPTING A GROWTH VERSUS FIXED MINDSET

You are ultimately in control of your identity — both its formation and upkeep. But having an identity is one thing; it's another thing entirely to keep evolving it. Because let's face it, change is uncomfortable. In fact, it is often frowned upon by others. 'You've changed … ' can be used as a deeply personal insult.

As it turns out, however, carrying a fixed identity can be quite damaging to our levels of happiness and fulfilment. World-renowned Stanford psychologist Dr Carol Dweck has studied fixed versus growth mindsets for 30 years and unpacks her findings in her book *Mindset: The New Psychology of Success*. Dweck shows that the differences between the two groups (fixed and growth) are remarkabl on just about every measure.

Those people who have a 'fixed' mindset believe that character, intelligence, talent and ability are set and won't change in significant ways, and assume that success is a result of inherent intelligence. On the other hand, a 'growth' mindset thrives on challenges. Failure is not seen as evidence of a lack of intelligence but as an opportunity to learn, develop new skills and grow. The following table provides some examples of the difference between fixed and growth mindsets.

Fixed	Growth
I've always been hopeless at maths ...	Perhaps if I get some coaching and dedicate a little more effort, I can improve ...
I never stood a chance in that interview ...	I'm gutted I missed the job, but I'll contact the panel chair to find out where I can improve ...
I can't help it. I've always had a really short fuse ...	I can keep my cool in certain circumstances; I'm sure I can learn strategies to do this more often.
It's hopeless. What's the point?	That certainly didn't go as planned. Let's sit down and learn from our mistakes so it doesn't happen again ...

Think about famous athletes hitting rock bottom after retirement, the countless examples of people winning the lottery and being broke only a few years later, or the cases of relapsing substance abuse. These are all examples of people who don't grow and evolve their identity as the climate changes around them. If you believe you're just a [insert label], it's highly likely that's all you ever will be.

Stepping into your new identity isn't about severing all ties with who you were in the past or turning your back on who you've been. It's your previous experience that shapes who you are now and the path you've found yourself on. Ignoring that does disservice to your present — it's like cutting off a limb and pretending nothing happened. Your focus is not on developing a brand new identity, but expanding your identity. Say 'thank you' to who you've been and what it's taught you as you welcome in the new you. Be present to this expanding identity and all its facets, notice the doubts as they arise and step into a growth mindset to expand what is possible for you. It's time to surprise even yourself.

Fear – can it be your friend?

Your palms are sweating, your heart is racing; it feels like everything is on the line and success all rests on you. What if you stuff this up? If you fail, you have no-one else to blame. What if you fail monumentally? And if it works, you have to make good on those promises.

Everything in you screams *Run! Hide! Abort mission!*

Fear is all-consuming. It takes over our body and our ability to think rationally and makes the future feel like light years away.

In business, so many of our decisions are made through fear. We can't be too daring in our marketing because we might get backlash; we can't treat anyone as particularly special because others might feel left out; and we can't recognise great achievement because everyone needs to be treated fairly.

Emma Isaacs, entrepreneur and CEO of Business Chicks, a globally expanding women's networking business, shared with me that she has what she calls a unique relationship with fear — and it's one we could all learn from.

She spoke candidly about not only being okay with fear but also actively putting herself in the way of fear. (I can almost picture her cutting fear off in her car and yelling at it to get in the back seat, pronto!) She describes actively putting herself in the way of fear by saying yes to more. For Business Chicks she drove more events than her team had ever done before; she committed to major venues and then had to work solidly to fill them; and she shifted her family to the United States to launch Business Chicks internationally. On all of these steps, fear came along for the ride.

For you, if fear shows up it's not a sign to play safe. Tune back in with your purpose, set into play your strategy to drive progress and use the energy and anticipation that fear can bring to propel you forward. The reality is whenever we step out into new territory and start to get creative — being in business, working as a leader, crafting a new direction — fear comes along for the ride.

Fear is what sits between the idea and the action. Being in Stand Out is a time of action and a time of transformation, which brings with it a time of uncertainty. Fear is right there with you. Every. Time.

In her book, *Big Magic: Creative Living Beyond Fear* bestselling author Elizabeth Gilbert suggests that we need to shift our relationship with fear. Fear is not something we need to 'kick to the curb' or 'punch in the face'. In fact, fear has served us well on many occasions: it makes us vigilant and means we get things done, and it saves us from taking a step into the suspicious dark alley. It's our ultimate protector.

Gilbert goes on to state that fear shows up every time we're doing something new, creative and uncomfortable. Its presence doesn't mean it's automatically in charge, though. Fear is an indication that we're pushing the boundaries, but we don't need to make decisions through fear. Gilbert sums it up expertly by saying 'Fear gets a voice but not a vote'. Being present to how fear turns up for you allows you to ensure your decisions are not being made by fear, and so ensure that fear doesn't blindside your trajectory. Sitting with the discomfort and vulnerability of change allows us to step forward into the successes of tomorrow. We revel in the story of overcoming. In fact, this is true for every hero's journey.

Every hero's journey follows a similar path, as outlined by author Joseph Campbell. Every hero's journey has a call to action, a series of trials and challenges before the fall into the abyss, followed by revelation, transformation, atonement to the adventure and a homecoming. Your journey into Stand Out is not dissimilar. You'll go through this hero's journey in a thousand ways on a thousand days. My call to action for you is to be present to the journey. Don't dismiss the abyss, because we only get to the revelation and transformation by going through it.

This is part of your beautiful story, and stories are what spark our hearts and minds. When we recognise this and can ride through to our awaiting transformation, we'll be ready to serve others more powerfully, boldly being present to what they need.

The curse of action for distraction

I was going to call this chapter 'Fail. Fail fast', and the intent behind that chapter title was good. I wanted to capture the idea of letting go of the fear of stuffing up, and instead ripping into the work and, when it doesn't work, picking yourself up and going again. Fail, learn, then rinse and repeat. I held onto this chapter title (and the idea behind it) right up until I came across this psychological bias that I instantly recognised in myself. The bias is known as 'action bias', and it means when things get complicated you get busy and into action, even if that activity is counterproductive.

When faced with uncertainty, your temptation may be to double-down on busy. 'Action bias' is an emotional reaction to the unsettling feeling that you should be doing something. For me, this is definitely true. When the stress hits a certain level, I turn into a whirlwind — and not in any kind of constructive way. I end up paying bills twice, delegating things that don't need to be done, and sorting out the kids' cupboards and throwing out clothes that still fit them and they still actually wear (not while they're in them, mind you).

THE MESS IS WHAT MATTERS

Don't get me wrong: being in Stand Out is busy. The returns on your efforts are great because you're making progress. But make no mistake — there's still effort, a tonne of it. But getting busier simply because you've hit complexity is really a distraction from sitting in the mess. We distract to avoid facing ourselves, and to avoid diving deep into the unknown.

The mess is where the magic happens. The moment we distract ourselves from sitting in the mess, we take ourselves away from the learning.

THE MESS IS WHERE THE MAGIC HAPPENS.

Striding into Stand Out is the greatest personal development ride you'll ever find yourself on. Put yourself out there and you'll learn things about yourself you never knew existed. Those things that press your buttons, and those things that shake the foundations of your long-held, oft-unhelpful beliefs. Some things you'll love and others you'll be embarrassed to admit even to yourself. The goal is to be present — to absorb this moment, pay attention to what is happening and get curious.

Notice your responses in this space and bring forth a scientific curiosity about what is happening. Put yourself back into high-school science, with your lab coat on. What did your teacher tell you when the results of an experiment you were conducting didn't match your hypothesis? You needed to get curious and enquire further. 'Isn't that interesting,' you might say. 'I wonder what is driving that? Where does that come from?' The same goes for being in Stand Out. Be present to your responses, the good, the bad and the downright ugly.

Curiosity, by its very nature, wants to be satiated. When we start enquiring, our brains scour the known and unknown to figure out what is happening. Imagine getting a random text message from a number you don't know. Imagine getting five of them in quick succession. Your curiosity is fired and it's nearly impossible to focus until you figure out who the messages are coming from. Use this insatiable drive to your benefit. Get curious about yourself and your responses.

Cultivating boldness

You can cultivate boldness, and so evolve your identity and be present to serve others, in three key ways:

1. *Pay attention:* notice what's changed and changing for you. In particular, pay attention to your responses.

2. *Be inquisitive:* rather than jumping straight into 'this is shit', pause and be curious about what's coming up for you. Notice when the wave of overwhelm and uncertain wash over you. Bringing curiosity rather than judgement to these moments changes their trajectory. 'Isn't that interesting' is a more useful attitude, tactic or strategy when facing change than 'F&8k! What the *bleep, bleepity bleep bleep!!*'

3. *Reach out:* we get caught in overwhelm when we're in isolation. Find people who you trust to share your experiences with, and reach out to others on a similar path to you who offer understanding and support.

Life hack: Toast the victory before the battle

This life hack shows you how to celebrate all that has got you to Stand Out state.

The idea

Folklore has it that during medieval times, the Vikings would gather the night before a battle and raise a toast to their impending victory. They were celebrating their achievements to get to this point, acknowledging the preparation that has happened and reinforcing their purpose.

Your battle might not be as defined or bloody, but when you step into Stand Out, you are nevertheless in a battle of purpose and progress. Celebrating what it has taken you to get there is not an understatement. We can be notoriously bad at ceremonies and rites of passage in the Western world, and we can learn a lot from the cultures and groups who do this well.

The action

1. Write down the thing that you are currently working on — that project, that big event, that goal.

2. Gather the people who are involved in it, even if they are your cheersquad

3. Celebrate and toast the success of this goal before it's finished. Celebrate in your style and honour the success of stepping up, regardless of the outcome from here.

CHAPTER 13
Do it your way

When it comes to living in Stand Out, find a way to 'do it your way'. (Kinda sounds like a line from a Dolly Parton ballad ... or is that Frank Sinatra? Whatever.) You need to battle conformity through your ideas. Turn up in a way you never have before and create a new way of operating. While we can learn patterns and lessons from others, this is your time to set the trend. Know what the non-negotiables are and then play with the rest. Give yourself permission to fly your freak flag and do it your way.

From trend-getter to trendsetter

In March 2015, Tom Goodwin published an article on techcrunch. com with an opening paragraph that caught the attention of many:

Uber, the world's largest taxi company, owns no vehicles. Facebook, the world's most popular media owner, creates no content. Alibaba, the most valuable retailer, has no inventory. And Airbnb, the world's largest accommodation provider, owns no real estate. Something interesting is happening.

These words have been shared, liked and—the ultimate compliment—turned into memes in various ways online and offline since Goodwin shared them. We live in interesting times, where our view of the way things 'should' be is being shaken up and challenged on a daily basis. And this is opening up the opportunity for us to examine our own thoughts of *It'll never work* — to challenge the default around the way we live, work and play.

Now, more than ever before, you, your team, and your organisation have not only the opportunity but also the platform to be a trendsetter in what you choose to pursue.

Disruption breeds innovation

Remember the last time you moved house? If you also needed to sell the house so you could move, you probably spent hours cleaning corners, scrubbing walls and making the place look its best to attract the highest bidder. You'd probably heard the research that having freshly brewed coffee in the kitchen and baked bread in the oven switches on the emotional centres in the potential buyer's brain and encourages a sale. So you spent Saturday mornings before inspections baking and brewing.

Furniture gets moved to places it's never sat before, shelves get decorated in new ways, and gardens get lovingly tended. After the hours of effort and sweat, you take a step back to inspect your handiwork and wonder why the hell you would ever sell a place that looks this amazing.

Disruption breeds innovation. When we disrupt the norm, the status quo, we start to see new ways of operating in our world that we previously hadn't paid attention to. Change gives us the opportunity to look through different glasses at everyday patterns. Through the growth of 'hackathons' (times when individuals come together to collaborate intensely to generate new products or processes) in our workplaces, organisations are going out of their way to disrupt things even when they are working well — because they understand that innovation and advantage are born out of uncertainty and change. Shifting into Stand Out is an internal and external disruption you are going through, so it's time to 'hack' your own habits, shake things up and try on new ways of interacting with your world.

DISRUPTION BREEDS INNOVATION. WHEN WE DISRUPT THE NORM, THE STATUS QUO, WE START TO SEE NEW WAYS OF OPERATING IN OUR WORLD THAT WE PREVIOUSLY HADN'T PAID ATTENTION TO.

Disrupt the natural patterns that we slip into, even for the small things. For me, disrupting how my day starts has been revolutionary. Instead of being sucked away from dreamy sleep by the pitter-patter of little feet and fingers prying my eyelids open each morning well before they're ready — and so being on the back foot for the rest of the day — I realised capturing the sacred solitude of time before the household wakes is integral to my sanity and my ability to tap into calm. Now I'm up at 5 am and my non-negotiable is ten minutes of solitude. This completely changes how I turn up to my day. Sometimes I'm out running at this time, sometimes I'm reading, sometimes I'm stretching, and occasionally I even have a bath (seriously, the pre-breakfast bath has changed my world).

So, instead of having dinner at the same time and the same place every night, mix up your routine by packing a picnic and heading to the river. Instead of booking back-to-back individual meetings with your team, look at catching up with people in duos so the conversations are still intimate while halving your time. Disrupting your pattern on the small things has the power to shift your world.

YOU HOLD THE RULE BOOK

The majority of our work at Pragmatic Thinking involves delivering presentations and training programs. Very early in our business, we decided to stop handing out the traditional training evaluation forms for the sessions we delivered. You know the ones because you've filled them in — asking you to rate the food, the venue, the presenter, and whether Tom's outfit matched the company logo or not. Ditching these forms was a conscious choice and one we haven't regretted, but it wasn't a natural shift to make.

We used the evaluation forms when we started our business, and when we sifted through them we started to notice a trend. What would happen is that we'd get 24 forms back with exceptional feedback, from people who loved and raved about the session. But then one person would make a note about the chairs being too hard to sit on for the day. And that would be the one that we'd obsess over and stress about. In that instant, all the other evidence faded and we would fall into the vortex of 'Should we have even gone into business? We should have known better, maybe we should start sewing chair cushions to hand out to people at every training session we ever run from here on in. In fact, I'll source some material this weekend and clear the decks for a Saturday crafternoon spree. Yep, that's the answer'.

This vortex was exhausting and unproductive.

Then one day we had a colleague run a workshop with our clients and we asked if he wanted us to print off his evaluation forms for him. He shook his head and said offhandedly, 'Oh, I don't use evaluation forms'. To say that our jaws hit the floor would be an understatement. So we politely asked, 'What do you mean you don't use evaluation forms?' His response changed how we ran training programs from that day forward. 'Whenever I get evaluation forms, I find myself consumed by the person who rated it only as "good" not "exceptional", and ignore the other responses that all raved about the session. I've realised that feedback in this context often says much more about the other person and what they're going through than it does about me and my session, so I stopped doing them.'

Whoa ... what? You're allowed to do that?

So we took it for a spin. At our next training program we didn't hand out evaluation forms at the end of the session, and guess what happened? Absolutely nothing. The floor didn't start caving in, the Earth didn't stop spinning on its axis. When it comes to rating how well a session went, we are by far our own biggest critics. We know when a concept or session has landed well and when it hasn't. And as far as getting feedback from our clients, well, we started asking them face to face what was of value for them. And we listened to what behaviours they changed, because their behaviours speak louder than any Likert scale can. Their re-engagement or referrals are the greatest feedback mechanisms we could get.

Just because it's 'what is done around here', doesn't mean that you have to keep doing it, particularly if it's not serving you or the people around you. We didn't stop getting feedback completely, but we stopped the method by which we received that feedback and stopped obsessing about the things that we had little control over. Instead, we focused our efforts on increasing our expertise in what we had complete control over.

You hold the rule book of how you operate. Fight a battle against the whispers of 'Oh, I can't do that because ...'. Remember Uber, Facebook and Airbnb, and consider what else might be possible in your world. Each of these concepts started with an experiment — they started with someone saying, 'Well, maybe we can. Let's give it go'.

Experimentation mindset

Have you ever been given really great advice and not taken it? We all know we should floss every day; in fact, research has found that if you had to choose between brushing and flossing your teeth, it's better for your dental hygiene to floss. But we're conditioned to associate clean with the minty fresh feeling and flossing isn't part of our normal routine, so we don't floss. We are surrounded by good advice and great ideas, but we don't put many of them into action.

One of the reasons is because of previous experience — where we tried something new but it didn't land for us. But these new ideas likely didn't work because we believed all we needed was the good idea — that is, if we simply put this idea into practice, it will automatically become our new ritual. And this works for a while. Our motivation is high for a couple of weeks. We're consistent about going to running group every Monday and Friday morning, and we have a week of eating chicken and salad for lunch every day. And then life happens. We've got to invest extra time in a project and so we skip a Friday morning running session. We have visitors stay for a week and the chicken and salad turns into chicken parmigiana. A month in and we've slipped back into old ways of operating. So we throw the idea out as one that just doesn't work for us.

To me, two more steps are needed in the process to shift a good idea to something embedded as a new ritual. My red-bearded friend Dr Jason Fox talks about the importance of running experiments. This forms the first step in shifting something from an idea to a ritual in our life. The second step involves committing to practise what we've learned. Let's step through each of these.

SET THE EXPERIMENT

The first step is to move the idea into an experiment. When we approach a new way of operating — when we start to embed our values into our life and take on board strategies to map out and see progress — we need to come to these ideas with an experimentation mindset (see figure 13.1).

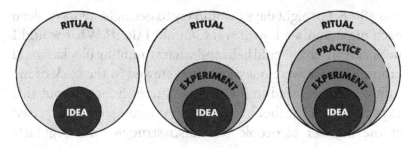

Figure 13.1: the experimentation mindset

Bringing a scientific approach to new ideas means that we start with a hypothesis (for example, 'I think going to running group twice a week would be great for me') and then we test the parameters of this hypothesis. Does it work every week? What happens when visitors are staying? What time of day works best for me and those around me? An experimentation mindset removes 'failure' from the equation and suggests that something not quite working the way we thought it would simply provides us with new data and an opportunity to tweak the conditions.

Last year I took on my own experiment. I'd just finished reading *Thrive* by Arianna Huffington (editor of the global platform *The Huffington Post*). Arianna calls out the importance of prioritising sleep in our busy world, recognising that putting off sleep is a flawed strategy if we want to be more productive, more successful and more healthy. Arianna talked about her own non-negotiable to get eight hours sleep every single night, which means turning down evening events and being conscious of not working late. At the time, I was deep into our business and had two small children. I hadn't had eight hours sleep for what felt like years. But if it was good enough for Arianna Huffington, it was good enough for me to try. I was intrigued about whether I could even do it.

So rather than just draw a line in the sand and say, 'That's it, I'm going to get eight hours of sleep every night from here on in', I decided to set myself an experiment. The experiment was #8in8. For eight days I would try to get eight hours of sleep each night and see how it went. Could I do it? What would I notice? And what would help and what stumbling blocks would crop up? These were questions that stewed in the back of my mind. I also decided to invite others to join me and put this experiment on Facebook and Instagram, completely surprised at the number of people who also struggle with regularly getting a good night's sleep.

I decided to start this #8in8 experiment on a Tuesday. Now, I've run fatigue hygiene programs, I've studied what you need to do to optimise sleep, and I did it all on that night. I'd figured out what time I would get up and what time I needed to be in bed to maximise the chance of a solid eight hours. I'd had a warm shower an hour before bedtime to kick in the cool-down trigger than precedes sleep, and unplugged from all screens and technology over an hour earlier. I'd had a sleepy-time tea, and done five minutes of deep-breathing. I was going to nail this.

At 9.30 pm I gave Darren a good night kiss, shut the bedroom door and jumped into bed to read for a bit before turning out the light (this was before I'd set the habit of getting up at 5 am). And then I tossed and turned for two hours as I struggled to switch my brain off. My faith was waning. *But it's just an experiment, so stick with it, Ali.* Eventually I got off to sleep, but at about 3 am I heard the sound of small feet come over to my side of the bed. My daughter tapped me on my shoulder and said, 'Mummy, I feel sick' and then promptly threw up in my hands — and I spent the next hour cleaning up. Needless to say, I didn't get my eight hours of sleep that night. But because it was an experiment and I'd committed to it for eight days, I stuck with it.

Over the next seven nights I stuck with the experiment with varying degrees of success. Certainly, on some nights I managed to get a full eight hours of sleep. While I didn't every night, this experiment had some side bonuses that I didn't expect. I certainly felt more rested and more energised, even if I didn't quite get the full eight hours. I finished reading two books, which usually take me months to churn through, and my quality of restorative sleep was greater.

As you look at new ideas and new ways of operating, bring along your experiment mindset and reframe what could be seen as potential 'failure' into a fascinating detour. To get the most out of your experiment, commit to these three rules:

1. *Set your experiment question:* what specifically do you want to explore? Make it clear from the outset, knowing that this experiment might change.

2. *Adjust the conditions:* things you can play with even during the experiment include:

   » *When:* mix up the times and days.

   » *Who (and who else can do this):* consider inviting others or recruiting the help of others.

   » *What:* change what you actually do; swap the sleep-tea for a peppermint tea, for example.

   » *How:* experiment with your mindset, your motive and your method.

3. *Commit to a time frame:* set a finite time frame to run the experiment, choosing something manageable that doesn't feel like forever. Consider eight days if it's something you'll do every day, or maybe three to four weeks if it's less consistent. Commit to the full duration regardless of how it goes, remembering you can tweak the question and the conditions, just not the commitment.

PUT IT INTO PRACTICE

Now that you've got feedback on what works for you and what fits into your world, it's time to put the idea into practice. This is a commitment to a longer length of time and the springboard to habit formation. Start with 90 days as a way to commit to the practice.

Do these two steps of experimentation and practise and shift that great idea into a ritual that specifically serves you and your needs and survives beyond Friday arvo drinks. Do this and these are the trademark behaviours that you can become known for.

TRADEMARK BEHAVIOURS

What do you want to be famous for? For who we are and the work we do to rise above the noise of our world, we can engineer our identity and our personal brand around trademark behaviours — things that people implicitly link back to us. Having Stand Out thoughts that are cutting edge are great, but they are nothing until we shift them into Stand Out behaviours. In chapter 7 we explored the importance of designing our behaviours around our values.

Embedding these behaviours even further can happen through creating a few key trademark behaviours that we become known for. What will yours be? It might be walking into work and giving people a high five each morning. Jonathan Thurston is a well-known rugby league player for the North Queensland Cowboys, but he has also become known for his trademark behaviours of always handing the kicking tee back to the ball boy after he kicks a goal, and giving his headgear away at the end of the match. These behaviours speak volumes on his value of respecting others.

In terms of organisational culture, American online shoe store Zappos is known for its unique recruitment offering. At the end of their induction process, they offer new recruits a $3000 cheque to leave the organisation, no questions asked. This has been a successful driver of culture and certainly one of their organisational trademarks. Explore what you want to be known for, and what your trademark behaviours are. The way to shift them from naff to genuine is ensuring they ring true to you — they need to be authentic.

Amplify your hidden trendsetter genius

Chances are you downplay things that you know because you assume 'everyone knows this'. An architect might instinctively know where to place a new bookshelf in their house, for example, while a designer instinctively knows what colours clash and what colours complement the outfit they put together for Friday night drinks. A wellness expert instinctively knows to grab for the water more than the wine on those same Friday night drinks. The thing is, though, these choices aren't instinct. These choices are informed by information — by the experience of having done these things time and time again, and by the reading and the research that sit behind these everyday, seemingly small choices.

Things that you've studied, observed, read about and absorbed in a way that no-one else has because of your experiences and who you are, these things are your genius. Scrutinise your hidden genius. Breathe life into those things that you know and assume 'everyone knows'. Amplify them, and your uniqueness will become embedded into everything you do. Bringing to life what you know others find valuable is the ultimate key to becoming a trendsetter.

SCRUTINISE YOUR HIDDEN GENIUS. BREATHE LIFE INTO THOSE THINGS THAT YOU KNOW AND ASSUME 'EVERYONE KNOWS'.

This is the perfect way to combat the trend-destroying question that lurks in the back of your mind: 'Who do you think you are?' You're a genius. When you bring what you know to the world in a way that invests in and serves others — that's when you Stand Out.

Fly your freak flag

When we live in a world where anyone can rent out their home to strangers across the globe, and it can all happen in 30 minutes without a single call centre or administration person, we really have the opportunity to change the game and how it's played. Let go of 'I can't because ...' As you embrace your uniqueness, remember to innovate with wild abandon. Consider this your permission slip to play, experiment and do things your way. Make no apologies for what you bring to the table.

Life hack: Take a curiosity walk

All too often we're so busy that we rush through our day and then, in the pockets of 'brainstorming' time, expect inspiration to turn up. Here's a life hack to find inspiration through curiosity.

The idea

It's easy to get caught up doing what others are doing without exploring new trends or new possibilities. What we need is a jolt that gets us out of our current experience, and gets us consciously noticing the ideas, metaphors and connections all around us.

Nature is an untapped resource when it comes to inspiration. Take a walk in nature, at the local park, around the lake or river, or through the bush, and explore the metaphors from the natural world.

The action

Take a curiosity walk for 20 minutes. You can either go somewhere you've never been (a street you've never walked down, a bush-track or a local park), or visit somewhere you go to regularly but look at it through the eyes of curiosity. Nature dishes up lessons upon lessons, from how things grow to how multiple organisms coexist. You can also start to notice the way nature and urban living environments collide and benefit. These insights can provide metaphors for a blog post, or ideas for your business.

If you are interested in exploring customer service, notice how a retail space designs its layout, notice how customers interact not only with staff but also with other customers. How does this place operate? Finally, ask yourself, 'What's working here that I could adopt or use?'

Schedule this observation time into your week.

CHAPTER 14
Gather your tribe

Breaking new trends, stepping into what truly matters, creating momentum, and being present to the mess, the confusion and the uncertainty of being in Stand Out can be incredibly isolating. Those things you could previously rely on, even if they weren't that great, are now shifting. As your identity starts to shift, so do your relationships, sometimes seismically. Put yourself out there and people will react.

In chapter 1 we spoke about the call to 'produce' — to 'bring into being' something that has your fingerprint on it and that could not exist the way it does without your influence on it. Nowhere in the definition of 'produce' does it say that when you bring something into being it has to be perfect. Worrying that we can only unveil something when we've worked solidly to iron out *all* the kinks is pointless.

Nowhere in the definition does it say that when you Stand Out you have to do it all alone. Yet we have an unspoken belief that whispers to us that none of our work counts if others help us, and that we have to suffer in silence and do it all to be able to claim the achievement. Our inner martyr rears its ugly head once again and stops us reaching out at the exact time that reaching out is what we need. But when we unpack it, genius *never* happens in isolation. It's these quiet beliefs that hold us back from living a Stand Out life. Unless we look them square in the eye and call them out.

From cut-off to community

The antidote to this misguided belief that you have to do it all? Gather your tribe. Shift from feeling cut-off to being upheld by a community — your community. You may find that you are gathering a 'new' tribe — a tribe that upholds you through the challenges of where you want to go. Find the community that becomes your rubber band, springing you forward (rather than the rubber band that snaps you back to the old).

SHIFT FROM FEELING CUT-OFF TO BEING UPHELD BY A COMMUNITY – YOUR COMMUNITY.

So that you can turn up and invest in others in a way that actually changes them (and doesn't just serve your ego), be purposeful about reaching out and gathering the tribe you need around you. If you're investing in others without having a community to support your vision and actions, you're exposed to the influence of uneducated criticism and the pull of 'needing to be liked'.

One of the things that I hear often from the people I work with and connect with is a yearning for a safe space to drop the facade and be themselves. I see a collective desire for this space. What I've realised is that every group, networking event and community is wonderful and flawed at the same time. Some will match exactly what you need right now, and others will leave you running for the hills to get away from these 'crazy' people. Your job is to create the safe space that you need for you — that safe space to land when the inevitable fall, critique and scrutiny come.

Figure out what you need and then connect with the right people for the right purpose at the right time. And if you reach out and they aren't the right people for now, don't stop the search. Just because that door didn't open on the crew you need today, doesn't mean they aren't out there. In an age of global connection people are waiting to be in your corner. Have the courage the pick up the phone, send the email, shoot off a tweet or unleash the carrier pigeon. You don't need to jump back into isolation. Rather than wallowing in the self-pity of 'no-one understands', get to work on gathering your tribe and creating the community you crave.

GENIUS DOESN'T HAPPEN IN ISOLATION

Do a quick experiment with me. Think about that very moment when Thomas Edison discovered the light bulb. What do you see? Where was he? How long had he been working away in the laboratory before the bulb finally lit up for that very first time and he realised he was onto something?

When I think about this moment, I see young Thomas absorbed in his work on his own. It's midnight, the empty coffee cups are piled on the bench near him and the bags under his eyes look like they're packed for a family holiday to Alaska. In that moment of light, when the globe glowed for the first time, I see him jumping up, sending coffee cups flying across the lab floor, and bursting out the doors, onto the street to call out 'Eureka!' to anyone who would listen.

We often believe that genius happens right before these 'Eureka' moments, when the scientist, the expert, the artist slaved away diligently in isolation before uncovering their genius onto the world. The grand 'Ta-dah!' moment that Hollywood movies are made of.

The reality is that all great inventions have been off the back of teams and groups coming together, and extending off other previous thinking and ideas. Edison had a team of over 30 people working with him on the light bulb work. The 'Eureka' moment was probably more like a team huddle and a round of awkward high fives. The collective collaborative effort shines the light in these moments (literally, in Edison's circumstance).

Collaboration with your tribe is what sits behind you living a Stand Out life. Those people who you've admired from afar may be the very people to help you in the next stage. Combat the belief that you've got to know all the answers. Ask yourself who can help you here, and then take a chance on reaching out to them. You might find it was worth the effort.

Reach out

It was a Friday evening. Nothing unusual about it — the end of a week of activity and the pull of the pause was calling me. The kids were tucked up in bed, so I poured myself my second glass of wine and sat down to watch whatever 1990's movie rerun was on the box. But the joys of running my own business mean that even in this scenario I never quite switch off, and it seems I wasn't the only one.

As I curled up on the lounge, I got a text message from someone I hadn't met but who had mutual connections through an Australian networking group called Business Chicks. The text said, 'Hey, Ali, you don't know me, but I've seen you pop up on Instagram a few times lately. What you do fascinates me. It would be great to connect with you'. Followed up almost instantly by another message that said, 'BTW, I never do this, but I've had two glasses of wine so I thought, why not?'

Aside from that sounding like something out of the rom-com movie I was about to watch I was struck by her courage to reach out. Of course, I replied with, 'I never do this either, but I'm matching you on the wines, so sure. How's next Wednesday sound?'

In a busy world where we constantly meet a multitude of people, how often do we truly reach out and connect with others? More and more people are craving the sense of belonging that comes from a close-knit community who just 'get you' and get what you're trying to do. You've got great mates and your family are supportive, but they don't really understand what you actually do.

Business can be a lonely place. The buck stops with you on the hard decisions and key choices. So we all want a place that is about more than just swapping business cards and practising our latest sales pitch. We crave a safe place to come together with other like-minded people to challenge each other, learn, grow, support and be supported.

But this sense of feeling 'cut-off' is not restricted to the business context. Whatever you're working towards — whether you're committed to raising a family, supporting local community endeavours, building your artistic portfolio or working in an organisation — can create this sense of 'it's just me'.

Magic happens when people come together in service of each other. We crave it. But then we sit back and wait for it to magically come knocking on the door or arrive via a text message on a Friday. What struck me was how incredibly rare this was. In a world where we are infinitely connected — where we know intimate details about people we've never meet — true community is rare.

MAGIC HAPPENS WHEN PEOPLE COME TOGETHER IN SERVICE OF EACH OTHER.

Here's the thing. No-one can create the ideal community that you need except you.

It's time to get over yourself and reach out to others to create the community you crave. I get that it's scary. In fact, the key reasons we don't reach out are these:

» *Reaching out makes you feel vulnerable:* it's scary because you're putting yourself out there. The other person or people might say no or not have the time. Or they might stretch and challenge you in ways you're not ready for.

> » *Reaching out costs:* it takes time, effort and sometimes money if you need to travel to connect with others. Are you prepared to give of yourself to pay these costs?

> » *Reaching out might not be worth it:* you might not have anything in common. It might be a waste of time. Be okay with this uncertainty, because it also may just be the greatest connection you ever made.

Despite these barriers, we need these genuine connections. The friend who tells you what you need to hear, not what you want to hear; the person who can see the very thing that's sitting in your blind spot; the perspective that you just couldn't get on your own. Without this, you and your 'why' go stagnant quickly in a fast-paced environment.

Stop waiting for the invite. You have permission to reach out and create the tribe that you want to be a part of, the one that will help you drive your goals for where you are at right now. The perfect community for you.

Reach out and there might just be someone else sitting at home on a lounge watching a 1990's rom-com who is grateful for the courage you took to contact them and say, 'Let's hook up'. Reach out and gather your tribe, because they don't know you're looking for them.

The right peeps for the right purpose

I can't give you a rule book on who you need to hang out with in order to fuel your Stand Out life. It's about finding the right people for the right purpose. Having said that, you do need three groups of people in your corner: the champions (those masters in their field), the challengers (those who stretch you and hold you accountable), and the cheersquad (those who are in your corner no matter what).

Reach out to these people, connect with them and find ways that you can serve them, and they'll repay you.

THE CHAMPIONS

All of us stand on the shoulders of giants — those people who've come before, whose thinking inspires or challenges our own. You can also think of these people as the masters. They may even be champions whose opinions you disagree with, but their thinking allows you to cement your perspective and get greater clarity on why this matters to you.

Your champions may be people you are fortunate enough to be able to spend face-to-face time with. Or they may be experts whose work inspires you from a distance; their influence shapes your thinking and approach. They may even be people who are no longer alive but their legacy impacts on you today.

Your champion list can be extensive and can be in an industry unrelated to yours, but these people still must affect how you interact with the world. Write down who they are and then find ways to devour even more of their stuff. It might be reaching out for a coffee with them, attending events or workshops they run, paying for mentoring with them or reading what they put out. Then teach others the lessons you've learned from your champions.

To expand your champions list, find out who inspires your champions and devour their stuff too. Read twice as many books, listen to more podcasts, and watch more talks (TED is a great place to start).

Take some time out now and explore your champions. Ask yourself:

» Who are my champions?

» How will I engage with them more?

» What do they teach me?

THE CHALLENGERS

The challengers are the people in your life who know how to give tough love. They have an ability to tell you what you need to hear, not only what you want to hear. We may not always want to hear what they have to say, but we need them to help us grow. You could also call them magicians.

They challenge for your good (not theirs), they are thoughtful when they give feedback, and they have a way of leaving you feeling respected in the process.

Before you dive straight into seeking feedback from anyone willing to give it to you, consider these rules around sourcing your challengers:

1. *They have expertise:* the people to pay attention to need to have a level of expertise in the area; otherwise, you're getting well-intended opinion but it's not necessarily helpful or relevant. If you want to be challenged around your financial status, seek out an accountant or financial planner, not your local barista. You may well have different challengers for different purposes.

2. *They understand where you want to be:* your challengers need to have an idea about the territory you want to step into and not be intent on putting their own agenda on your direction. If you want to talk about the state of your relationship, talk to someone in a 40-year marriage that's going well, rather than your friend who's going through a divorce.

3. *They're completely present for you:* true challengers are the ones who are present for you without being distracted by their own agenda. And if they do provide advice that is more about them than you, they have the self-awareness to come back and call that out. They know how to check in and make sure the challenge lands for you.

As you gather your challengers, be wary of the well-meaning advice-givers. Those are the people who will give you their opinion, whether you ask for it or not. And this advice can come from the delusion of expertise. We all have it. For me, it emerges when I'm watching a grand slam tennis tournament. From the comfort of my lounge, without a single piece of tennis expertise, I become the armchair commentator on what the players need to do. Don't they know if they just served and volleyed they'd have won an hour ago!

It's these armchair experts we need to be wary of. Seek instead to invest in the advice of those who both know what they're talking about, and have your best interest at heart. When it comes to gathering these people ask yourself:

» Who are my challengers?

» What areas in my life are seeking to be challenged more?

THE CHEERSQUAD

These are the people who are absolutely in your corner, celebrating your every step — the people who are there with the bubbly when you succeed, and the brainstorming session when the setback sets in. You may call them your mates. Your cheersquad is authentic, organic and almost embarrassingly over-the-top. I'm talking the frantic fanatics here, not the polished cheerleaders.

If you think about cheerleaders at sporting events, they are (usually) perfectly in sync and highly manufactured. Their outfits are engineered, their poses are overly practised. Cheerleading is a sport — they train and when it comes to game day, they deliver. But once game day is done, they pack up their pompoms and head home.

The kind of cheersquad you want is the passionate fanatic in the stands. The one who lives for the game, and when the final whistle is done they are still shouting the win from the rafters. You want the rebel on the hill who is unashamedly passionate. Your cheersquad needs to be just a little bit crazy and delusional about how awesome you really are.

As you move into Stand Out, your cheersquad may evolve. Doing the thing that lights you up and having the courage to set boundaries can be incredibly confronting for some people. Perhaps people you thought were in your corner slip out the back door when it comes time to blow the final whistle. That's okay.

You'll have different cheersquads for different purposes. My dad is my number one fan. He's proud of everything I do and is incredibly supportive. In fact, I couldn't do what I do without his support — it's phenomenal. And yet, most of the time he's got no idea what I do. And that's okay. Others in my cheersquad understand the depth of what it takes to get up, turn up, and show up in the kind of work I do. Gather your work squad, your family squad, your relationship squad, your art squad.

Who are the people in your cheersquad?

Invest in others

Your champions, challengers and cheersquad are your others. Invest in them. They can absolutely be the same person, but they may not. Don't be afraid to pay for their time. You might be one of the lucky few who can find someone in your social life who fulfils all these roles. If you can't find someone to fulfil these roles for you, source them and pay for their time. Typically, it's the challengers that we don't spend enough on. We don't engage in (or with) the people whose opinions, given specifically for our context, can shift us significantly. By investing in them, you'll invest in your future self.

Gather your tribe at the start and they'll be there to celebrate with you at the end (and along the way). It starts with asking for help.

ASK FOR HELP

Asking for help is scary. It's confronting. It can feel like 'giving up' — like the final straw to admitting that you can't do it all on your own. And yet until we allow ourselves the vulnerability to truly ask for help from others, our growth and influence will be limited. You can't (and you won't) do it all solo. Drop the facade and ask for help.

When I say it's time to ask for help, I don't mean the 'Oh, it would be nice if you could, maybe, possibly, but I don't want to intrude ...' type of hinting for help. I mean looking the person in the eye and saying, 'I need your help'. If this comes naturally for you, brilliant. Keep it up. In fact, stretch further — you never know when your request will open doors you previously thought were only for those with the secret code. But if, like a lot of people, you struggle to ask for help, this barrier is one that needs confronting.

Start by asking yourself what beliefs you have about asking for help.

Maybe you see it as a sign of weakness? Maybe it's something that others do but never you? *Never.* Maybe asking for help requires you to be honest that you can't do it all on your own? Maybe you see asking for help as social suicide or vocational suicide?

Asking for help is not a sign of weakness.

People want to be a part of your compelling 'why'. They want to contribute to your bigger vision and be inspired by what is possible. Asking them to support you and help you doesn't diminish their 'why'; it doesn't impose on them or drag them away from what they want to do. In fact, contributing to your bigger vision fuels their 'why' with inspiration and possibility, because helping you creates a sense of belonging and connects them to a tribe that is there to cheer them on too. Give them the joy of helping — if you don't, you deny others sharing the journey with you.

WHEN YOU STAND OUT YOU GIVE OTHERS PERMISSION TO DO THE SAME.

It might sound like all you need to do is have the courage to ask and the rest will be all roses, sunsets and mojitos. But that may not always be the case. In fact, that won't always be the case. When you reach out and ask for help, others may say no, or they may say yes but then not deliver (which can feel worse). It's not a given that they will drop everything, organise the parade and wave the banners to cheer you home. If they say no, it's not a reason to demand a refund on your friends. Often it's not about you and is more about what's going on for them. And that is totally okay. Remember their boundaries are as important as yours. Honour them for sticking to what's true to them.

Trust others enough to ask them for help. Respect them enough to allow them to say no. Trust yourself enough to cope. Love yourself enough to keep asking.

Remember — when you Stand Out you give others permission to do the same.

Create your community

Here are some tips for creating your tribe:

» *Be clear on what you want to learn:* just saying you want to connect with other cool peeps is not enough. Be specific.

» *Ask:* the reality is that other people are craving the connections and learning that you are.

» *Find your challengers:* be open to seek out people who will stretch you and your thinking. If you go for the safe options, your goal to grow may not be met.

» *Be vulnerable:* share what scares you and what you need help with.

» *Come together with generosity and gratitude:* go into these connections with the mindset of sharing with others the things that would be of value for them.

Life hack: Double your consumption

Here's a life hack to stretch yourself and your network through doubling your consumption.

The idea

Get gluttonous on great ideas by consuming those things that will stretch your thinking and expand your network. Double your consumption of books in the field that you are pursuing, and double your consumption of conversations in this area.

The action

Here are a few ideas on how you can double your consumption:

» Write down the top five experts in the field you are pursuing and reach out to them.

» Read the leading books in the area you are interested in.

» Subscribe to the blogs of the experts you admire and get consumed by their work.

(continued)

Life hack: Double your consumption *(cont'd)*

» Join a group. Share your questions with others and be immersed in conversations and ideas. If you can't find the group that juices you up, connect with the people whose thinking inspires you and invite them for a coffee.

Whatever your main pursuit — be it health, career, speaking or _____ (fill in the blank) — double your consumption.

This is your time to #standoutnotalone.

Stand Out wrap up

This is the sweet spot and the toughest terrain you've faced to date. Exploring what will shift for you in this state is key to sticking with it through the mess. Finding ways to move from blindsided to bold, from trend-getter to trendsetter, from cut-off to community will be the supports you need to live a Stand Out life. As you do, make sure you come back to these three key actions:

1. *Be present:* this is the time to stop and breathe. Being present to the clarity of your purpose and having awareness of the progress is equally as important as being present to the mess in the success. Be curious about the shifts for you; know that every great story and transformation comes with sticky moments. Be present and bold in yours.

2. *Do it your way:* now more than ever we live in a world where disruption is breeding innovation. Focus on your values, the skills you have and your unique perspective to have the courage to create your own trend.

3. *Gather your tribe:* genius doesn't happen in isolation. Gather the champions, the challengers and the cheersquad that will be in your corner as you live this incredible Stand Out life. Have the courage to reach out and ask for what you need. Give others the honour and the joy to be a part of your amazing journey.

So, where are you at?

Look at where you are now across these elements, then jot down what drags you back to the left side, and what sees you leaping and bounding over to the right. Now zoom in on the areas you want to focus on.

FROM   **TO**

Hit reset button
MARTYR ———————— — ——— **WARRIOR**

Reestablish boundaries
VICTIM ———————— — ——— **VALIDATED**

Reconnect with what matters
CYNICAL ———————— — ——— **GRATEFUL**

Values - Define what's important
OBSCURE ———————— — ——— **CLEAR**

Design a values-aligned life
DIMINISHED —— ———— — ——— **AMPLIFIED**

Defend the sacred
EXPOSED —— ———— ———— — **PROTECTED**

Progress - Map it
BLINDFOLDED —— ———— ———— **BLUEPRINT**

Progress - Chunk it
IDEA ———— ———— ———— **ACTION**

Progress - See it
HIDDEN ——— ———— ——— **VISIBLE**

Be Present
BLINDSIDED ——— ———— ——— **BOLD**

Do it your way
TREND-GETTER ——— ———— **TRENDSETTER**

Gather your tribe
CUT-OFF ———————— — ——— **COMMUNITY**

Conclusion

Feeling overloaded is all-consuming. Holding back the tide of busy is exhausting. For me, the drive to write this book came from the men and women who I connect with on a daily basis. In the quiet, safe space of our conversations, when busy paused for just a moment, I would hear their despair and witness their fatigue. Behind their eyes was the belief and hope that things could be better. That it had to get better. That their efforts could make a difference — and not just a little one but a seismic one. This was where they found the drive to keep getting up and turning up, even among the busyness. But the 'pushing through' came with costs and collateral damage. Costs to their happiness and relationships, significant costs to their health, and costs to their belief in themselves. They were losing sight of the best things that life had to offer. All this work and no play, they would question — for what? With each cost their shoulders drooped just a little further. These stories resonated with me, because they reflected my own despair and heartache. Their story was my story.

Diving into researching this book has allowed me to come back to the importance of starting with self, and the realisation that the best time-management strategies in the world are pointless if we don't have a strong sense of who we are and what matters to us. Productivity tips, as brilliant as they are, can actually add to the overload if we don't have the courage to set clear boundaries. Doing more is not the answer. What fascinated me, though, was that clarity of purpose, while important, is also pointless on its own. Without action and momentum, dreams stagnate and can turn to resentment. When two drivers are combined, magic happens: 'Why this?' (*purpose*), and 'What's next?' (*progress*) are both needed to live a Stand Out life.

I wrote this book to help you gain clarity around both of these drivers of change. One of the greatest gifts you can give those around you is to be clear on your core self. Get clear on what matters to you — because, as international communications expert Michael Grinder says, 'When you know your core you can face both fame and failure and not be swayed'. I have this quote written above my desk at work and it's my recentring when busy rattles the cages again. Take that strength of knowing your core and turn the dial up on your ideas. Look for the glimmers of what excites you, of where your curiosity or intrigue go when you are daydreaming. It's now your responsibility to put effort, energy and weight behind these glimmers. What would happen if you moved beyond, 'Oh, it would be nice to ...' and put that idea on steroids? Move it to the crazy extreme that frightens even you, the place where your internal cynic tells you it's never going to happen. That's where I want your purpose to sit. In the tension of, 'Oh crap — yes, let's do this'. Don't just build a business to replace your salary. Ask yourself, what would happen if it was on the world stage? Don't just lead your team a little bit better, build a reputation on excelling at leadership. And don't just believe that it's important to help the person next to you, empower them to help others too by creating a movement.

The way you bring these ideas into reality is to obsess about making progress. Move yourself into full-blown Freak Out and then focus on the processes that will start moving you forward. Come back to focusing on the next steps. Progress is a foxy little minx, though, because it can come disguised as a setback. Picture these little setbacks using the imagery of a tick. We've got to test the waters on the road that didn't work, taking the downward line on the tick, in order to leapfrog onto the pathway forward, the whoosh and flourish of the upward movement on the tick. Keep reaching out, keep asking questions and keep driving forward. Stick with it; your montage of triumph is coming. Because so many opportunities are available to us when we lift our heads above the noise.

We are infinitely abundant in the resources we have at our disposal. In 2014 I was fortunate enough to travel to Malawi with a charity group called The Hunger Project. The work that The Hunger Project did on the ground and their tirelessness in shifting the mindsets of those in poverty to take responsibility for their own prosperity were some of the most inspiring things I've had the fortune of witnessing. In particular, I remember meeting a 76-year-old lady, Lily, who only 10 years prior had taken out a microfinance loan to purchase some pigs and start her business. At the age of 66 she became a business woman. This was a woman who had endured over six decades of hunger and poverty, and a number of famines. Her resourcefulness to step up and say yes, to see the abundance she had, which most of us would see as so little, meant that when I sat with her in the red soil of Malawi I got to see the pride on her face. The pride as she showed me her 20 pigs, her two cows and her hut that she built. And the pride as she shared that she is now fully self-sufficient and cares for her four grandkids. Lily is my guide in the uncertainty. She is my reminder that we have enough and we are enough.

Returning home from this trip I recall talking with a friend who was struggling to make ends meet, who was battling the busy of a corporate world, and was drowning his sorrows at the local bar most weekends as he could see no way out. The contrast of these two stories hit me. We have so much possibility at our fingertips. Use what you have, bring who you are and make progress. This is not just a 'nice to have'; it's not just a sweet, cute thing to aspire to. It's not even just something that you ought to do. It's actually your responsibility. It's your role.

Your voice matters. Without it the world misses out on another perspective, the person next to you misses out on making a connection, and the people you serve miss out on the learning. It's your job to call things out that aren't right. It's your role to have a clear 'why' and create momentum that others can follow. Playing small serves no-one. In fact, it dishonours those around you — it dishonours your biggest supporters. Don't just do it for you. Do it for those who don't have a voice. Do it because not having your voice contribute to the conversation means that others miss out. Do it because your story matters, and the story of the person next to you matters. Do it so that you can role-model to the person next to you, the people in your team, the next generation. Show them what amazing things might be possible if you work to pursue a Stand Out life

Quit the judging. Stop the editing. Own it and step out into it.

Find purpose in the process (unlock meaning in the mundane) and find processes around your values (the things that your heart gets drawn to). This work has been a coming back home. To me, the biggest message from this work is that you have permission. Permission to be you. Permission to write the next chapter — however you want to write it. Permission to reconnect with the very best of humanity, even when you are sometimes faced with the very worst of it.

This is what I believe:

I believe that everyone deserves a safe space just to be.

I believe in celebrating and lifting each other up.

I believe that when we have the confidence to share our story, the world shifts (and the world loses out when we don't).

You have greater capacity for influence than you can imagine. And when we come together to learn, laugh, cry, question and grow, and, in doing so, step back into the world with the belief that we are messy, imperfect and brilliant, and that we are enough, then anything is possible.

Your actions create shock waves. Small behaviours lead to big opportunities. We don't do it just once. We turn up every day and say yes to the mess. Because when you look around you this life is messy, imperfect and brilliant. This is what I want to say yes to. This is my pursuit. This is my call for you.

Boss of busy planner

Before you tie a ribbon around this book, I'm obsessed about making sure that your desires don't gather dust alongside the baby photos under your bed but, rather, are strung out and crafted like award-winning Christmas light extravaganzas for all to see.

The anticipation of a new start is filled with excitement that makes your skin tingle. Not bad tingle, like stinging nettles, but good, goosebumpy tingles. Is this the moment to bite the bullet and finally make that change? Could this be the year??!!

Anticipation has a flip-side, however, and it kicks in when the excitement hangover wears off and the promise of beginnings quickly falls back into the mundane routine of washing up and red lights.

You feel a sense of deflation. You know, the same feeling you get when your favourite character on *The Bachelor* doesn't get picked at the rose ceremony. Or when you stock up during the Boxing Day sales with stuff that you soon just know will fuel your garage sales of the future. Short-lived excitement, followed by hall-cluttering regret.

So, what's going to be different in the coming months?

The one key difference between the things that stay as an idea and those that get transformed into reality is this: **you work on them.**

And this is where the real work starts. Within psychology I know that the right question at the right time has the power to prompt you to think differently and to see something you haven't seen before — and this can be a game changer. Planning out your 'why' and your 'what's next' will be the thing that keeps you moving towards Stand Out.

This planner is filled with questions to help you do just that. It is designed for you to send the kids/partner/puppy/boss out to play, pour yourself the beverage of your choice, cosy up in your favourite sunny spot with a pen and get to work.

This planner is your intention zone; your place to honour those hidden desires, to be curious about what is actually holding you back (it's often not what you think it is), and to come back to when life throws you a curve ball. Life will pull you in a million different directions this year if you let it. The way to combat that, and to stay steadfast on what's important to you, is to get clear on your intention for the year.

Don't let what happens next happen by chance; engineer it in a way that it happens by choice.

Here's to making sure you #standoutnotalone ('cos everything's better in hashtag).

> There is no better **time** than now.
>
> There is no better **idea** than this one.
>
> There is no better **person** than you.

The great, the grind and the grateful

Before we focus on what's ahead, let's squeeze the last lessons out of the previous 12 months. Let's start by focusing on the great, the grind and the grateful:

» *The great:* write down all the great moments of the past 12 months that come to mind.[1]

» *The grind:* take a bit of time to reflect on the moments throughout the past year where you felt stuck in a rut and write them down. What did you learn about yourself in these moments?

» *The grateful:* what were a few things that surprised you over the past year? Write them down. (And I don't mean the kind of surprises where you find a pube in your soup, but the good kind. The kind that leave you feeling grateful.)

What did you endure in the past year that showed you how strong you really are? What strength did you find that you didn't realise you had?

What did you let go of in the past 12 months?

What will the past 12 months stand for?

Take the time now to write down your responses in all of these areas, and then to say thanks and farewell for the past 12 months before we welcome in the year ahead.

Au revoir

---

1   You know, like that thing that Uncle Bob did at your grandma's birthday party. *#hilarious #bobbiecanrap*

The year ahead: one word

Over the past five to ten years there's been a growing discussion about creating a word for the year ahead, instead of wasting time on resolutions we won't keep. Experts such as Gretchen Rubin, Ali Edwards and Dr Jason Fox talk about this approach and have all added to the collective conversation of the concept. I first came across this idea from designer and visual storyteller Ali Edwards, and for the past three years it's become an annual ritual with friends.

Some of my words for the past few years have been:

» unleash

» flirt

» warrior.

Ones that I've loved from others include 'magnet', 'launch', 'clean' and 'style'.

Thinking ahead, what is one word that you want the next year to stand for? Choose something that is aspirational, and something that kind of scares you when you say it out loud. Take some time to sit with your word. Often it finds you more than you having to force it.

Once you've landed on your word, take the time to think about how this word comes to life in different areas of your life — from relationships and work to finances and health.

Epic questions

The following questions will get you thinking about actions and opportunities for the year ahead.

COMBAT CHECK OUT

If you feel yourself drifting towards Check Out, ask yourself:

What do you need to let go of before you dive into the next 12 months?

_____   _____   _____

What do you want to make sure you don't ignore over the next year?

_____   _____   _____

In what ways is fear holding you back?

_____   _____   _____

What are the ways that you are going to hit the reset button?

_____   _____   _____

What are your non-negotiables for the year ahead?

_____   _____   _____

Who do you need to be firm about your boundaries with?

_____   _____   _____

What strengths are you going to amplify and hone in the next 12 months?

_____   _____   _____

What nurtures your soul?

_____   _____   _____

Sit with these questions and jot down your responses.

BATTLE BURN OUT

Among the busyness, what tracks do you need to lay down now to make sure you continue to focus on your health?

Write down one thing you could do to prioritise:

sleep

movement

nutrition

digital detox

Also write down how you're going to defend your health priorities when things get busy.

RAMP-UP RITUALS

At times throughout the next year you'll need to ramp things up — to give more and bring the energy required for the outcome you crave. Take the time to write down the 'ramp-up rituals' you can tap back into throughout the year. For example:

- What daily or weekly rituals work for you to ramp up your energy? (Loud music and singing in the car is always okay.)

- What (or who) helps you reconnect with your purpose?

- What songs, quotes, sayings, images or photos energise you?

REST-UP RITUALS

You'll also have times where you'll need to rest up and replenish — to take time out, switch off and just breathe. Before you hit the bottle for your quiet saviour, write down your 'rest-up rituals'. Committing to these may be more important than your ramp-up rituals. For example:

- What daily or weekly rituals help you to feel focused and centred among the chaos?

- How do you need to look after yourself when you are overloaded and stressed?

- What are the ways that you can hit the reset button?

- What is your 'fire-drill' plan in case the coming months kick you to the curb and you find yourself facedown in mud on the side of the road? (Metaphorically, of course.)

FOCUS IN FREAK OUT

If you feel Freak Out coming, find focus by asking yourself:

- » What have you got to rip into and stop procrastinating about?
- » How are you going to visualise your progress?

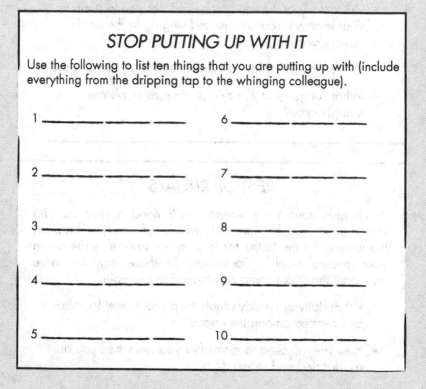

STOP PUTTING UP WITH IT

Use the following to list ten things that you are putting up with (include everything from the dripping tap to the whinging colleague).

1 _____   6 _____

2 _____   7 _____

3 _____   8 _____

4 _____   9 _____

5 _____   10 _____

Now put an asterisk (*) next to three that, if you got them sorted, would free up a heap of time and headspace. Imagine yourself not having to deal with that thing anymore ('Hawww!' I hear you say. 'Is that really possible?' Yep, I think it is — and it's imperative that you take care of it.)

Now write down your action plan for what you are going to get sorted and by when. Then make it a priority.

Goals that rock

Use the following to jot down the goals you'd like to achieve in each of these areas. (*Note:* Each of these is just a small box for a reason — goals should be short and snappy. Put simply, if they need copious explanation, they need better refining.)

Career and finance	**Physical health**

Family and friendships	**Mental health**

Travel and adventure	**Spiritual health**

Community support

90-day sprints

Get more specific and write down when you will tackle your goals across each of the four quarters ahead. Find your focus points in these 90-day chunks:

Quarter 1

Quarter 2

Quarter 3

Quarter 4

STEP INTO STAND OUT

To prepare to Stand Out, ask yourself:

- » What does being present mean to you?
- » What's your special sauce? Or what's your freak flag you're going to fly in the coming months?
- » What parts of your personality are you going to amp up, step into and own?

The people who matter

Use the following table to write down specific people who you want to connect more with in the outlined areas.

The Masters	The Magicians	The Mates
(The champions, experts, gurus, all-round legends you want to rub shoulders with)	(The challengers who sprinkle pixie dust on your ideas, who tell it like it is, who leave you feeling different after a chat)	(Your cheersquad; the ones in your corner, who remind you what's important, and know when to bring the champagne and tissues)

Who do you trust with your stuff?

Whose opinion actually matters to you? (And whose really doesn't?)

Fast-forward 12 months

Shoot yourself forward to 12 months from now and picture what you've achieved and where you are at in your life.

In what ways did you #standout this year?

What amazing things did you step up and do that you never thought you could?

How are you feeling about the incredible year that you've had?

And, lastly, the big question ... what are you doing to *celebrate*??

This is your year
- make it epic

#standoutnotalone

Acknowledgements

Cliché's like *'it takes a village'* exist because it reflects the truth that a book like this doesn't come together without a significant tribe of people sitting, pushing and driving the project to come to life. The champions, challengers and cheer-squad who sit firmly in my corner are extensive and I'm blown away and grateful for every single one of them, those acknowledged here and those I've missed and who I'm just as grateful for having in my life.

This book moved beyond being simply a model and an idea when Kirsty Mitchell grabbed my shoulders, shook me a little and exclaimed, *'you've got to write the book'*. Thanks for the not so subtle prod Kirsty, and for your unwavering support of all that I and our team do. The coalition of the awesome have a world to go and shake up, thanks for being one of the drivers.

Lucy Raymond, thank you once again for taking a chance on this idea, and for believing in the concept not only for book shelves, but also for your own world. Thank you to the team at Wiley for your hard work to bring this book to life, and to the beautiful Charlotte Duff who made the editing stage not only painless, but actually enjoyable. Your words of encouragement were my elixir.

The majority of this book was written in the early hours of the morning while I took up a booth at our local café, Good Day Coffee. To DJ, Ebony and the team, thanks for letting the weird girl in the corner tap away in your space while you kept the almond latte's flowing.

To my cheer-squad tribe who dropped everything when I sent up the flare in the midst of this project. In particular Keri Krieger and Jen Jackson — your ability to help me see the trees while I was lost in the forest, battling the inner war of self-doubt, made this book even better. So grateful for who you are and who you stretch me to be.

Thank you to the troops who continue to inspire, push the boundaries and drive me to be bigger every day, including the brains of Jason Fox, Kim Lam, and Dougal Jackson. To my amazing team at Pragmatic Thinking, the world has just started to see what talent you have and can't wait to share this adventure with you. Kym Davis, my right-hand designer, who helped me to rattle the cages of design within these pages. I love the result.

Within this book I talk about the importance of gathering your tribe. I'm grateful for communities like Business Chicks and Women in Focus within whom I've connected with life-long friends and influential women who inspire me every day.

To my clients and to you the reader who are courageously stepping into living a Stand Out life. You encourage me and inspire me to continue this work in my own life. Thank you for your bravery.

Family is my grounding place; from my extended family who shaped who I am today, to my own family who remind me daily what matters, thank you. Especially to Pat and Kate for laughing at my daggy dancing in the kitchen and for your patience while Mum was busy 'writing her book'.

Of all of this gushy love, my biggest gratitude and love goes to the person who sees me at my worst and still says *'I choose you'*, my husband Darren. Your DNA is threaded throughout this book, it is what it is because of your talent and ideas. Your belief in me floors me every day, thanks for pushing me beyond every boundary I set for myself.